The OC Heart Diet

The OC Heart Diet

By

Lawrence J. Santora, MD
Steven A. Armentrout, MD
Dick Butkus

Cover: Art design by The Graphics Company.
Cover photo rights: Lawrence Santora MD.
www.ocheartdiet.com
www.arrowhead-classics.com

ISBN 1-886571-19-8
EAN 978-1-886571-19-8

Second Edition: February 2006

10 9 8 7 6 5 4 3

Contents

Aknowledgements

EBCT technology has been considered one of the greatest tech-nological medical advances of our time. However, it was up to a number of medical pioneers to put the technology into focus as a means to save lives. Despite much skepticism by the medical community in the early days of EBCT coronary calcium screening, these pioneers forged ahead, sometimes against significant criticism, to develop answers through arduous research that are now the basis for using this unique lifesaving technology. Matthew Budoff, MD, head of the EBCT Imaging Center at Harbor-UCLA, is one such pioneer who shared his vision, knowledge, and belief in this technology, not only with us in Southern California but throughout the world. In the past, he was often a voice in the darkness, now arguably one of the world's leading authorities on EBCT technology and coronary calcium screening. We would like to thank him for unselfishly sharing his knowledge and vision with myself and other latecomers to the field.

We would also like to thank a friend and colleague, Gerald Friede, a talented researcher, who, while at The Cooper Clinic, developed many of the early studies on EBCT technology that now stand as the basis for predicting cardiac risk and helped bring

EBCT scanning to the clinical forefront. We appreciate the many years he spent developing the nuances of EBCT technology and developing outstanding programs in EBCT coronary calcium screening and CT angiography and sharing his expertise with us.

We would also like to thank Blair Braverman and John Lehner for their contribution to new concepts in diet and exercise.

Special thanks go to Rina Santora, RN, for the many hours she spent reviewing this manuscript and her many creative ideas in bringing this book to fruition.

Lawrence Santora, MD
Steven Armentrout, MD
Dick Butkus

Introduction
to
The OC Heart Diet

Do We Really Need Another Diet Book?

The *OC Heart Diet* is not just another diet book. It is a detailed roadmap for a lifestyle program that is comprehensive yet simple to follow. You will maintain an ideal weight, feel better, look better, and live longer! *The OC Heart Diet* is for all ages. It will prolong life and prevent deaths from America's number one killer: Heart Disease.

The Roadmap -
Three Intertwined Components

It starts with a remarkable and unique technology to detect heart disease. The EBCT heart scan is a relatively inexpensive simple, noninvasive test to determine if you have heart disease. If you have heart disease, the diet and exercise program will prevent it from progressing. If you do not have heart disease, the program will prevent you from developing heart disease.

A comprehensive dietary program that is simple, effective, and easy to maintain for a lifetime, the program will help you lose weight, and then maintain your ideal weight based on the latest scientific principles. The results are astounding! You will have more energy, better endurance and recovery time, and improved muscle mass, as well as serving as a great anti-aging component. This weight-loss and maintenance program will control almost all the major risk factors for heart disease.

The third component is an exercise program that is tailored to the individual. It is easily modified from the simplest walking program to a more detailed program that has been shown to improve the performance of even elite athletes.

How to Use This Book

The diet and exercise program in The OC Diet will help a person of any age group. However, if you are *having any symptoms* of heart disease—chest discomfort, shortness of breath —or any unusual symptoms that occur with exercise, like jaw, arm, throat, or back discomfort or chest burning that occurs with exertion, you should *see your physician before using this book.*

• If you are without symptoms and simply want to start a program that will allow you to reach an ideal weight, feel better, look better, and live longer, then follow this approach:

• If you have never been known to have heart disease (that is, you have never had a heart attack, a coronary stent or balloon angioplasty, or coronary bypass surgery) and have at least one risk factor, or no risk factors but want an assurance about whether you have heart disease:
   a. Arrange for an EBCT heart scan.
   b. See Appendum A for the location of the latest EBCT center in your area.
   c. Make sure that your heart scan is performed on an EBCT scan and not just a conventional CT scan.
   d. See the following chapter to understand the difference in the types of CT scans. This is very important.

- If you have no coronary calcification (hardening of the arteries) on your EBCT scan, follow the diet and exercise portions of this book after consulting with your doctor.

- If you have coronary calcium, you should follow the diet portion of this book, but check with your doctor before starting this exercise program and also for recommendations for starting appropriate medications to prevent the progression of the disease.
- If you have had a heart attack, a coronary stent or balloon angioplasty, or coronary bypass surgery, the dietary program will be beneficial for you. The EBCT scan has benefits even in these settings to follow progression of the plaque, but you should get the EBCT with the guidance of your doctor. The exercise program should only be done with the approval of your doctor.

Part I

There has been an explosive growth in technology and our understanding of heart disease over the past twenty years. The rate of heart disease is growing in part due to the aging population, however, the survival rates from heart attacks are improving due to application of our advanced technology. The key to making inroads on this growing epidemic is to apply this amazing technology for the early detection of heart disease, then apply the latest medical, nutritional, and exercise approaches on an individual basis.

Part One of this book offers exciting and vital information that can save your life.

1

Early Detection of Heart Disease
and
The OC Heart Diet

T he *OC Heart Diet* is a simple plan for saving lives from heart disease. The key is early detection of heart disease. Early detection of heart disease allows a treatment plan that will slow or reverse heart disease in those of highest risk. If you already are known to have heart disease, the diet and exercise program, with the approval of your physician, will help prevent further progression of your heart disease.

Early detection of heart disease allows a treatment plan that will not only save lives, it will also save money. Our present national resources are stretched thin. Care will be rationed as costs soar. Presently, we treat people with medications that do not need them, yet we do not treat people that do need the medications! How can this be true?

It is true! We are misappropriating our healthcare resources. What happens when we treat people with medications that they don't need? We waste money. We subject patients to the side effects of very powerful and expensive medicines that may not be necessary. What happens when we don't treat people who do need

3

to be treated? They die suddenly from heart attacks or wind up needing coronary bypass surgery or intra-coronary stents.

The OC Heart Diet allows you to take charge of your life, take charge of your heart, and take charge of your healthcare dollars. This approach has the potential to save many lives and untold millions of healthcare dollars. *The OC Heart Diet* plan will allow us to live longer, more productive lives by preventing heart disease and making more healthcare dollars available for other disease conditions—other social situations. The federal dollars are all intertwined. It is not a stretch of the imagination that if billions of dollars spent on heart disease can be redirected toward other social issues (for instance, preventing childhood disease, more funds for education, etc.), there can be a real change for good in our society.

The OC Heart Diet is based on twenty-five years of clinical cardiology practice, extensive cardiovascular research, and the use of the latest technologies to detect and treat heart disease. *The OC Heart Diet* is a plan that brings it all together in an easy-to-understand, step-by-step approach to detecting heart disease, what steps to take if heart disease is detected, and then applying exercise and dietary programs that are based on scientific evidence. *The OC Heart Diet* is a roadmap to a long, productive, and healthy life. The diet and exercise program will benefit anyone of any age, even if they do not have heart disease.

My cardiology practice has encompassed all aspects of heart disease during the past twenty-five years. Like most physicians trained in cardiology, I have been amazed by the explosion of new technologies and medications to treat heart disease after it develops!

I have been doing invasive heart catheterizations and coronary angiograms for twenty-five years. Invasive coronary angiography was developed over forty years ago. It is a very exciting technology that allows physicians to identify severe coronary artery disease. Prior to invasive angiograms, there was no reliable way to visualize blocked coronary arteries in such a way that the area and the severity of the blockages could be identified.

Once angiograms were perfected, methods were then devised to repair the arteries with coronary bypass surgery (also referred to as open-heart surgery, which can encompass not only fixing the arteries but also, though less common, the valves of the heart). Coronary bypass surgery is now a well-established surgery, performed by *cardiovascular surgeons* (not by a cardiologist), that saves lives and relieves chest pain. Almost 400,000 coronary bypass surgeries are performed each year in the United States.

By the late 1970s, early 1980s, less invasive catheter-based techniques were developed as an alternative to coronary bypass surgery. The initial catheter technique was balloon angioplasty, also referred to as PTCA. This was and still is a valuable alternative to fixing the blockages in the coronary arteries in certain patients. The coronary arteries have to have a blockage in a certain area of the artery to be suitable for the catheter techniques (a catheter is a small tube inserted through the artery in the leg or arm, through which we inject dye to visualize the coronary arteries on the surface of the heart.).

The catheter-based techniques are far less invasive than open-heart surgery because only a small puncture mark is made in the artery of the leg or arm with local anesthetic and mild intravenous sedation. Obviously, this has great appeal to patients since the hospital stay is only overnight, and there are no incisions and subsequent scars on the chest, as occurs with open-heart surgery. Coronary angiograms and fixing arteries with catheter-based techniques are performed by cardiologists, not cardiovascular surgeons.

All cardiologists have an internal medicine background, with additional training in diagnosing and treating all forms of cardiovascular disease. The training includes interpreting and performing various types of cardiac tests, like echocardiograms and stress testing. A *noninvasive cardiologist* performs all forms of cardiac treatment and testing, except for invasive coronary angiograms. Cardiologists who in addition perform coronary angiograms are called *invasive cardiologists.*

Interventional cardiologists are cardiologists who perform coronary angiograms and also fix the arteries with some catheter-based technique. We are also involved in the usual treatment and testing performed by noninvasive cardiologists.

For twenty years I have been performing coronary interventions, successfully treating blocked arteries with small balloons (called balloon angioplasty) and intra-coronary stents (little slotted tubes that are inserted in the narrowed portion of the coronary artery). Today, intra-coronary stents are used far more commonly than balloons, lasers, or cutting devices. Coronary stents save lives and relieve chest pain (angina). They have become the mainstay in treating heart attacks.

As amazing and useful as coronary bypass surgery and coronary stents are, I realized many years ago that it is better to prevent heart disease than to treat heart disease after it has developed. It became clear to cardiologists that we needed ways to identify those at risk for heart disease and to treat it with the appropriate medications to prevent the need for coronary bypass surgery or stents. Although I continue to perform interventional cardiology, many interventional cardiologists like me became interested in *preventive cardiology.* Dr. Matthew Budoff, a fellow cardiologist and leader in the use of EBCT scans for coronary calcium screening, put it into perspective when he presented the following old Chinese adage:

Superior doctors prevent the disease.
Mediocre doctors treat the disease before evident.
Inferior doctors treat the full-blown disease.

It was clear to me that we were treating *"full-blown disease"* because our patients had advanced heart disease and needed open-heart surgery or coronary stents. We knew that perhaps we were also mediocre doctors (according to the adage) because we were treating many patients *"before the disease was evident"*. My goal—and that of many cardiologists—was to be superior doctors and *"prevent the disease."*

You might wonder: Isn't it a contraindication to be a *preventive cardiologist* and an *interventional cardiologist?* Wouldn't we put ourselves out of business if we prevent disease? Won't we run out of patients to put stents in? Not likely. The amount of heart disease is vast. Most physicians, contrary to popular belief, are not motivated by profit but by intellectual curiosity and doing well for their patients. Cardiology is a particularly demanding profession, with long nights, little sleep, and a storm of new technology that is forever challenging us to keep up. It is the most exciting of all the medical professions, demanding a blend of bedside diagnostic and history-taking techniques with the most advanced wave of technology of any medical field.

The OC Heart Diet is a culmination of that journey to be a *"superior doctor"*. The journey started in the early 1990s when medications became available that were powerful enough to reverse or control the progression of coronary heart disease, the major cause of heart disease and death in this country and in all industrialized nations. These medicines are the well-known *statin* drugs used to control cholesterol. A huge number of scientific studies overwhelmingly showed that they saved lives and reduced the risk of heart events by about 30%.

There was one particular patient that changed my outlook on treating heart disease. She was a 30 year old woman, diabetic for 20 years who I first met when she presented to the emergency room with a heart attack. Having a heart attack at age thirty is extremely uncommon, especially in women, however when heart disease does occur this early in life, it is often in diabetics. I went on to perform a coronary angiogram and found one of her coronary arteries to be significantly blocked. I fixed this artery with balloon angioplasty. This patient also had slightly elevated cholesterol of about 220 (which in 1985 was not considered that abnormal). She was unable to tolerate the cholesterol medications available at the time (mainly, immediate release niacin, gemfibrozil and cholestyramine), statins were not yet available. Six months later she returned with chest pain. Coronary angiogram revealed a second coronary artery now developed a new blockage, not present six months earlier. I fixed this artery with balloon angioplasty. Eight months later, she develops chest pain again, coronary angiography revealed both arteries that had been fixed earlier now had narrowed, plus her third coronary artery unbelievably developed a significant blockage. This time she went on to a three way coronary bypass surgery at the age of thirty-two. As unbelievable as it seems, within the year, two of her bypass grafts closed. I fixed both with balloon angioplasty. Around this time Mevacor (lovastatin), the first statin medication for high cholesterol, became available. She was started on Mevacor and did not have a subsequent cardiac problem for twelve years. These blockages were like a malignant form of coronary atherosclerosis (hardening of the arteries). We now know that the statins have many mechanisms of action in addition to the cholesterol lowering properties. They reduce inflammation of the arteries and stabilize the plaque. I imagine it was the anti-inflammatory properties that so dramatically change her course.

The lesson I learned was that *it is better to prevent heart disease than to try and fix it when it becomes fully advanced.* Finally, a treatment that did control atherosclerosis—but not in everyone! Statins are fantastic medications, but why did they prevent disease in only 30%, why not 60% or 90%? What else is causing heart disease?

What other risk factors are missing? These "missing links" have, in part, been identified and are discussed in detail. Who might have these other risk factors? Who should get the additional tests? How are these risk factors treated? All these questions are answered later on in the following chapters. Answering these questions for the individual is important in getting the maximum benefit from *The OC Heart Diet.*

Conventional Risk Factors

- Family History
- Diabetes Mellitus
- Elevated LDL Cholesterol
- Tobacco Use
- Hypertension
- Obesity/Physical Inactivity

These risk factors only explain about 65 percent of heart disease. What explains the rest?

It is a disturbing fact that only half the people with heart attacks have elevated cholesterol. So, cholesterol by itself is not a reliable risk factor to follow. Worse yet, now we had an effective treatment against cholesterol, but not everyone with high cholesterol develops heart disease! Do we treat millions of people with high cholesterol to prevent heart disease in half of them? The costs of this approach are staggering.

So, now in the late 1990s we had a great medication to treat cholesterol—we could be great *"mediocre doctors"* as the Chinese adage goes. We were able to treat people with high cholesterol effectively with medications "before the heart disease became evident." We also had wonderful intra-coronary stents, a dramatic improvement over plain balloon angioplasty (PTCA). Stents are safer and more effective and longer lasting than PTCA. Many patients who normally would need coronary bypass surgery could be treated with stents. Now we had the tools to be great *"inferior doctors,"* according to the adage. We were able to treat the "full-blown disease" very effectively. But how do we become *"superior doctors"* and "prevent heart disease?"

The technology emerged in the late 1990s to detect coronary disease: *EBCT* heart scans for coronary calcification. EBCT scans are special high-speed CT scans that are so fast they can take pictures of the coronary arteries of the moving heart in a matter of minutes, and all non-invasively. No hospitalization is needed.

If you think about it, taking pictures of the heart is much more difficult than taking picture of other organs (like the lungs or liver, for instance). The heart is the only organ that never stops moving, so all testing techniques for the heart have unique challenges. The emergence of the EBCT scanner is an amazing diagnostic test that had the unique ability to visualize the calcified plaque in the moving heart, all without placing any catheters in the body and doing it in mere minutes.

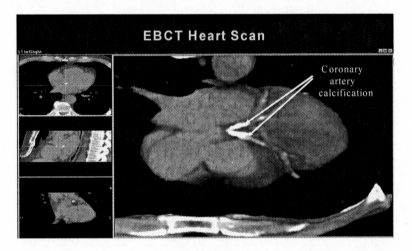

EBCT Heart Scan

It has long been known that plaque starts out as a soft cholesterol streak in the lining of the coronary artery (called fatty streaks). In time this irritant to the lining of the arteries goes through a healing phase and calcium is deposited in the soft plaque, forming a composite calcified plaque. What a lot of physicians do not understand is that there is always soft plaque between the calcified plaque. The more calcium that is present, the more soft plaque there is lining the artery wall. It is the soft plaque that can suddenly rupture into the opening of the artery.

As is usually the case, the plaque is not large enough to narrow the artery opening, so there are no symptoms until there is a small fissure or rupture of the surface of the plaque. At that point, a clot forms, closing the artery totally, resulting in a heart attack.

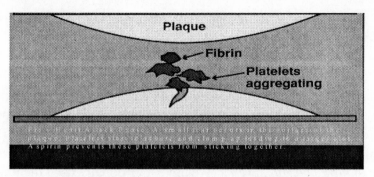

Aspirin prevents the platelets from clumping together

This sudden closure of the coronary artery by the ruptured plaque is what causes a heart attack (that is, heart damage). This sudden closure of the coronary artery is what could lead to sudden cardiac death. The calcium deposits are healed soft plaque that now have become hard plaque. The calcium can gradually narrow the artery over time. This gradual closure can lead to angina (chest pain) that may need a stent or coronary bypass to fix. *The bottom line: calcified plaque causes angina, the soft plaque cause heart attacks.*

The EBCT scan non-invasively detects the calcium. Quite simply, if you have calcium in the coronary arteries, you have coronary atherosclerosis—that is, hardening of the coronary arteries. You have the most common type of heart disease, the type of heart disease that is the leading cause of death in the United States: you have *coronary artery disease.* You might not have symptoms, but you have heart disease that could lead to sudden, complete closure of the coronary artery.

When you identify this calcified plaque at a stage before it narrows the artery, treatment with the proper medications, diet, and exercise can prevent the plaque from progressing, and even cause it to regress. What's more important, all the soft plaque in between the calcium can possibly be reversed and stabilized with the same diet, exercise, and medications that are described in *The OC Heart Diet.* If treatment is initiated early enough, rupturing of the soft plaque can be prevented. Heart attacks can be prevented.

Early detection is the key! Early treatment with The OC Heart Diet will save lives!

When the EBCT reports first came out in the 1990s, most physicians did not know what to do with the results. Many renowned physicians still do not know what to do when calcium is reported on an EBCT scan. However, a number of subsequent scientific studies have shown that coronary calcification is the *best predictor of future cardiac events.* We have traditionally used the traditional risk factors to predict the odds of a person having a heart attack. Coronary calcium is a fantastic addition to the traditional risk factors in determining your risk for a heart attack.

Based on the number of these risk factors that you have, we then determine who should be treated with medications to lower cholesterol. The cholesterol is then lowered to a certain range determined by your risk for a heart attack over the next ten years. The risk factors are called the Framingham Risk Factors, based on the results of following people in the town of Framingham, Massachusetts.

Based on this ongoing study starting in the late 1940s (and still ongoing), it was determined that people with certain levels of blood pressure, cholesterol, physical activity, smoking habits, and blood sugars were more or less likely to develop heart disease. Thus, guidelines were developed to modify these risk factors. Your risk of a heart problem is predicted based on the combination of risk factors. However, the risks give us a *prediction.* You may have none of the risk factors and still have heart disease, or you can have all of the risk factors and never have heart disease.

The EBCT scan tells you either you do or do not have heart disease! The quantity of calcium determines your chance of having a heart attack and how you should be treated. Depending on the quantity (if any) of coronary calcium, diet and exercise may be all that is needed; or if the quantity of calcium is high, medications, diet, and exercise may be needed.

The OC Heart Diet carefully lays out the roadmap. Though invasive angiograms and intra-coronary stents are here to stay, and are a busy part of my practice, EBCT scans finally provide an inexpensive, fast, safe, and accurate method to detect and treat early heart disease. Early detection and treatment with diet, exercise, and the appropriate medications will cut down the need for invasive angiograms, coronary stents, and coronary bypass surgery. The EBCT heart scan can save lives.

The new millennium brought a coalition of events for me as a cardiologist. A wealth of new data on cholesterol and other risk factors has come to light, a wealth of new studies demonstrating the usefulness of EBCT heart scans, my own involvement with my own clinical practice using EBCT scans and research using EBCT scans. In addition a dramatic increase in our knowledge about diet and how it affects heart disease and new theories on exercise methods and heart disease. There now existed the triad that we were looking for:

- A safe, noninvasive, inexpensive method to detect coronary disease in patients without symptoms—The EBCT heart scan
- Effective medications to treat risk factors
- New ideas on diet and exercise

Three other events now brought the concept of *The OC Heart Diet* to fruition:

- The detection of plaque in my own coronary arteries using the EBCT heart scan.
- Meeting legendary NFL Hall of Fame football player Dick Butkus (a patient and now a friend) who tells a remarkable story of an athlete with few heart-risk factors and no symptoms, who, at the suggestion of a friend, went on to have an EBCT scan which, without a doubt, saved his life. His involvement with exercise was one of the co-development factors in the exercise portion of *The OC Heart Diet.*
- Revolutionary and comprehensive diet program for preventing heart disease, co-developed for *The OC Heart Diet* with a friend and fellow physician, Dr. Steve Armentrout.

So, *The OC Heart Diet* will place you in charge of your healthcare. You will learn all about early detection, EBCT scans, and other appropriate heart tests. You will learn how you need to modify your life if necessary, what types of medicines to take or perhaps to avoid. A simple but scientifically based exercise program that is individually tailored for the couch potato as well as the elite athlete. A comprehensive dit plan, which is not really a diet but a way of eating that is easy to maintain for life. The *OC Heart Diet* will giv eyou the best chance of keepign your coronary arteries clean, as well as living a full and invigorating life. Also profided are comparisons of other diet plans, as well as advice on dietary supplements and follow-up testing. Live lokng and live well!

2

Do We Really Need to Die
of Heart Disease?

Heart disease is an epidemic. It affects a broad range of age groups and all socioeconomic classes, women as much as men. You are never prepared for an attack. Not to diminish the catastrophic consequences of cancer in a person's life, heart disease kills more people than all cancers combined. Unlike cancer, the effect of heart disease is usually often sudden and deadly.

These are the facts:

- Half of all heart attacks occur without warning; one's first knowledge of heart disease is often sudden death!
- Half of all heart attacks victims die suddenly—no time to ponder the situation, no second chances.
- Half of all heart attack victims have normal cholesterol.
- In the US, every thirty seconds someone has a heart attack in the US; every minute someone dies from a heart attack.
- In the US, people suffer 1,200,000 heart attacks per year.

- In the US, 500,000 women die of cardiovascular disease each year.
- More woman die of heart attacks than from all cancers combined.
- In the US, 400,000 coronary bypass surgeries are performed per year.

So, we ask the question: "Do we really need to die of heart disease?" Obviously, the answer is we are all going to die from something; presently, half of us will die from heart disease, most often in the most productive years of our lives. However, we can delay the clinical onset of heart disease or prevent heart disease completely with a judicious plan, which would include the following:

- Identify heart disease before it causes symptoms.
- Treat patients who need treatment with the appropriate medications.
- Avoid treating patients who do not need treatment so they can forgo medications and the associated cost and inconvenience.
- Save healthcare dollars so they can be used to treat other diseases and further research for cardiac disease.

The OC Heart Diet addresses all of these issues and gives a clear picture of what you can expect through testing and careful adherence to an appropriate diet and exercise program as outlined in *The OC Heart Diet.*

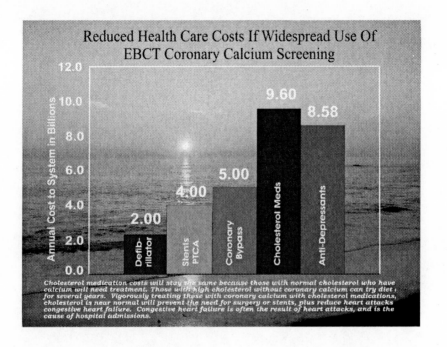

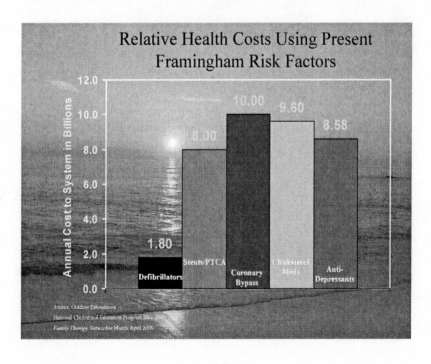

Dick Butkus - NFL Hall of Fame

3

The Dick Butkus Story

Dick Butkus, considered by many to be one of the greatest football players of all time, is an excellent example of heart attack prevention. His story is a compelling example of the benefit of early detection of heart disease and the amazing variation in the importance of risk factors in causing heart disease. Although he had one of the most extraordinary sports careers of all time, his lifestyle growing up can only be described as relatively ordinary for most Americans, probably not much different than thousands of other Americans who develop heart disease each year.

The commonly known heart-disease risk factors are an important contribution to our understanding of coronary heart disease. The Dick Butkus story, however, demonstrates just how much we really have yet to learn about coronary disease. Why can one person have all the risk factors and never get heart disease, and another, like Dick, have no or few risk factors and get heart disease?

- *How important is a family history of heart disease?*

Dick was the youngest of nine children, none of whom were known to have heart disease. His parents died in their 80s. They had no history of heart problems. Dick developed serious heart disease by age 57, leading to the need for coronary bypass surgery.

- *How important is diet in causing heart disease?*

Dick had the average American diet for his time: fruits, vegetables, meat and eggs, few processed foods or junk foods. His diet was probably not much different from other readers of this book who are in their 50s and 60s. He did have one unique dietary trait as he describes it. When he was a child, his Lithuanian heritage brought him foods as "Lithuanian rye bread with bacon grease or bacon bread with chunks of bacon and grease."

- *How important is sedentary life style in causing heart disease?*

Dick was an avid athlete since his grammar-school days, involved in all sports: handball, water polo, swimming, basketball, baseball, and (of course) football. Most sports in the later years were played to keep him in shape for football and to build his agility for football. He never had a weight problem.

- *How important are high blood pressure, high cholesterol, diabetes, and smoking?*

Dick was never a significant smoker, other than an occasional cigar. His cholesterol, untreated, was slightly above 200 at the time of surgery. He had normal blood pressure at that time and he never had diabetes.

So, despite having few (if any) risk factors, Dick developed significant heart disease. His cardiac-risk profile is probably not much different than that of thousands of typical Americans seen in doctors' offices every day across the United States. Most of these patients go untreated because the traditional risk factors are few (if any), and there are no symptoms. The real compelling story is that if Dick had undergone an EBCT scan in his forties or even at age 50, calcium and plaque would have been found and treatment started early enough to prevent or slow progression of his heart disease. He probably could have avoided coronary bypass surgery by having started early medical treatment. *Early detection of heart disease is the key!* Only an EBCT heart scan for coronary calcium has the ability to reliably and non-invasively detect early heart disease.

I first met Dick Butkus in the summer of 2002. At that time I had been practicing cardiology for over twenty years. I was part of a large cardiology group in Orange County, California. Southern California is a unique part of the county, not just because of its near-perfect, year-round weather and beautiful environment, but for three other reasons. Orange County is the home of a vast number of biotech companies, an unusually high standard of living, and a high proportion of hospitals doing cardiovascular procedures. In addition, EBCT scanning was introduced very early in Orange County, compared to other parts of the country. By the time I met Dick, EBCT scans had been entrenched in Orange County for at least ten years and had gained some notoriety from the Oprah Winfrey show in the late 1990s.

At that time, EBCT scanning was performed by radiologists. Radiologists are physicians who are trained in the interpretation of various types of x ray tests. Oprah Winfrey had a scan performed at one of these imaging centers, and the whole concept of EBCT scanning was briefly brought to the forefront of health news. Unfortunately, what was not brought to the forefront was what to do with the results of an EBCT scan once it was performed and evaluated.

The question was, "What should the patient and the doctor do with the results of the scan?" This was the missing piece of the puzzle. This is a very important piece of the puzzle that makes the test meaningful. After all, what good is it to do a test if it the results are not used to change how the patient will be treated?

To bring clinical benefit to the scanning, cardiologists around the country began to get involved with the interpretation of EBCT scans because of their clinical background in treating heart patients. The cardiologists were best suited to make recommend-ations on the indications for performing the scans and recommend-ations on how to use the results for a treatment plan for the individual patient.

Like many cardiologists, I followed the development of EBCT scans through the years, and by now I was convinced that it was a unique and powerful tool to detect and treat heart disease. I became convinced that it was one of the greatest technical developments in treating cardiovascular disease. I was also convinced that *prevention is the most important aspect of cardiology.* We now had a tool and the clinical research to back up the usefulness of this tool: the EBCT heart scan. Many EBCT scanning centers throughout the country developed clinical programs centered on the EBCT scan as a screening tool. The programs, like the one described in *The OC Heart Diet*, provide a treatment and educational plan based on the results of the scan.

Dick Butkus came to the EBCT imaging center at the recommendation of a friend of his who was a patient of mine. Dick lived just north of Los Angeles, at least a good hour's drive to the imaging center. I had heard of his football exploits most of my life and, like many people, considered him probably the greatest football player of all time. However, I was surprised to find him one of the nicest and most considerate people I had ever met.

His friend made arrangements for his EBCT scan. As Dick relates it, he was not mentally prepared for testing. He was not fully aware of what the test involved. Two days before his EBCT scan, he went to Death Valley in August, where the temperature is over 100 degrees in the shade, to play golf and to work out.

As usual for his workouts, that day he wore a rubber jacket and pants to enhance sweating during exercise. However, the heat that summer day exceeded 100 degrees making the rubber workout suit a little too much even for him. However, the fact that he could work out in the summer desert heat that day without any cardiac symptoms made the results of the upcoming EBCT scan even more unbelievable. After his trip to the desert, he showed up for the heart scan the following day.

Dick came to the imaging center with this close friend who also had the heart scan done immediately before him. The heart scan takes less than five minutes to perform. There is no special preparation. You are fully clothed when the test is performed. You lie on the table, hold your breath for less than thirty seconds, and the test is complete. His friend's scan was entirely normal. This provided some reassurance to Dick that his probably would be normal, especially since he felt well and was able to exercise in the desert heat.

The normal heart scan shows a faint outline of the heart's arteries as they lay on top of the surface of the heart. Plaque that is calcified shows up as white specks within the faint outline of the coronary arteries. With an increase in plaque, the specks join together and form white clumps in the arteries.

Dick's heart scan was clearly abnormal. His scan showed very dense white calcified plaque throughout all the coronary arteries. I knew after examining the scan that it was not going to be fun discussing these findings with him.

I remember the sinking feeling I felt when I first saw the scan of my own heart several years earlier and found calcium in my arteries. Seeing your own arteries in a scan is a completely different emotional experience than if a doctor shows you the results of your treadmill stress test. The EKG from a treadmill stress test looks like a bunch of unfamiliar squiggly lines on paper. Your heart scan looks like a heart. The coronary arteries that you see on the scan look like arteries. You can immediately identify with the scan. That's what makes it such a motivating test to modify behavior. You see white plaque in your own heart, and you instantly realize you have to change something in your life: you think of changing your diet and lifestyle.

Dick describes his experience with the scan like this: "My friend had his scan first. His was normal, so I felt confidant that mine would be normal. The scan took only a few minutes. After the scan I met the doctor to discuss the results. He explained to me how plaque forms in the arteries and how the coronary arteries function. He explained that as the plaque builds in the arteries, there can be closure of the arteries. He explained that the plaque shows up as white blotches on the heart. I said, 'Okay, no big deal, at least not for me.' When the doctor put up my scan, I saw five big blotches on my heart. 'Okay,' I said again. Then realizing I was seeing large chunks of plaque in my heart, I said, 'Oh no, this can't be true!' I was told by the doctor that the plaque on the scan does not necessarily mean that there is restriction of blood flow, but the more plaque the more likely there can be restriction of blood flow; and the more plaque, the higher the chance of having a heart attack. The doctor asked me, 'When was your last stress test?' I told him, 'I never have had a stress test in my life!'

That same day, Dick was tested on a stress-echocardiogram (a more accurate type of stress test tan the standard EKG treadmill stress test) to see if there was obstruction of flow in the coronary arteries. His stress test was only borderline abnormal, however when considered together with the very abnormal EBCT scan, I felt he needed an invasive coronary angiogram.

The invasive coronary angiogram is done in the hospital setting. Mild intravenous sedation is given, and the skin over the artery in the groin (the femoral artery) is numbed with Lidocaine. Then a small tube, called a catheter, is inserted into the artery and directed into the coronary arteries. A standard x-ray dye is injected with a syringe through the catheter. A camera over the chest records digital movie of the dye flowing through the coronary arteries. This is referred to as a coronary angiogram. We performed the coronary angiogram the next day. Two of the three arteries were totally blocked. The blockages were too extensive to treat with balloon angioplasty or coronary stents. Dick underwent open-heart surgery the next day and had five-vessel coronary bypass. He was discharged from the hospital in three days.

Dick went on to an uneventful recovery. He has intensified his cholesterol management and diet control. After his surgery he has became a staunch supporter for early testing for heart disease using EBCT scanning.

Dick's experience is not the usual course for patients having a scan, but it is not that uncommon either. Though a large percentage of patients who come for a scan are found to have plaque, often the plaque can be treated with diet, exercise, and medications.

There are many lessons to be learned from Dick Butkus' experience. Anyone can have severe life-threatening blockages and little or no symptoms. Anyone can have few (if any) of the traditional risk factors for heart disease and still have severe life-threatening blockages in the coronary arteries. It is also important to remember that it is often this mild plaque, which can suddenly rupture, causing a clot to form over the ruptured plaque, resulting in a heart attack. The stress test is usually normal and no symptoms usually occur until this mild plaque suddenly ruptures.

As a matter of fact, most heart attacks occur from plaque that does not restrict blood flow. It is important to understand this distinction. Stress tests pick up advanced plaque that is restricting blood flow. However, most heart attacks occur from the moderate plaque that does not yet restrict blood flow. So, the stress test is often normal and no symptoms are present until there is sudden rupture of the plaque. The EBCT is the only way to non-invasively (meaning, we do not need to insert any catheters in the body) identify this plaque and treat it appropriately with medications to prevent it from rupturing. Cholesterol medications cause the plaque to become firmer, smoother, and less prone to rupturing, even before the cholesterol levels decrease. We call this *plaque stabilization.*

4

Heart Disease Knows No Bounds

The epidemic of heart disease can touch any one of us. Heart disease touches the famous and the infamous, men and women, all races, colors and creed. Princes, paupers, and even presidents are afflicted by heart disease. President Clinton is the most recent and notable victim of heart disease. Unfortunate that he had such advanced heart disease, but fortunate that it was discovered before he had a heart attack or sudden cardiac death. He was able to have coronary bypass surgery, and he has returned to a normal, active life. Would an EBCT scan have been helpful for President Clinton? I am sure at this stage of his heart disease, the scan would have been extremely abnormal. However, since he had symptoms, a stress test was performed and was the preferably test to do at that stage of his heart disease.

However, throughout all the press and news coverage of his illness, the question was asked again and again, "How could the President of the United States have such advanced heart disease and have it go undetected?" What were the answers? Invariably, interview after interview with various experts, the response to that question was that he had no symptoms and his stress tests had been normal. The responders would go on to say that there was no way to detect his heart disease without a coronary angiogram. They would then add that a coronary angiogram was not indicated since he was without symptoms and he had normal stress tests. No one—not one expert—mentioned an EBCT scan. He was a perfect candidate for an EBCT heart scan when he was in his forties or even when he was 50 years old. He had high cholesterol and was in the age group where early detection could have made a difference.

I am very sure that if he had an EBCT heart scan at age 50, President Clinton would have had significant amounts of calcium in his coronary arteries that would have prompted vigorous cholesterol management. I am also sure it would have been a significant motivator to change diet and exercise habits. I believe this type of advanced disease could have been prevented or at least the progression slowed significantly. Again, *the point is to detect heart disease early!* Heart disease affects paupers, princes and yes, even the President of the United States. It certainly is wise for every President to have an EBCT heart scan.

Some celebrity stories are less fortunate than President Clinton's: the Darryl Kyle, John Ritter, Bobby Hatfield stories. The saga of cardiac death: it knows no boundaries. Daily reports in every newspaper in America report the death of a celebrity, a sports figure, a titan of industry—all die suddenly, no warning, no foreknowledge that what was to befall them was preventable.

Heart disease crosses all socioeconomic and ethnic boundaries. It is disturbing to me that with all the wealth and knowledge and access to the best care in the world, so many smart, successful, and talented people die from a disease they never knew they had the potential to have. But there are lessons to be learned from this. We have the technology at last to detect heart disease early and prevent heart attacks and the need for surgery.

Darryl Kyle, a 33-year-old immensely talented athlete, father, and husband, died suddenly. Autopsy showed extensive narrowing of his coronary arteries.

It is unusual to die at age 33 from coronary disease, but not unheard of either. Were there clues to this potential disaster? Could it have been prevented? We try not to be a "Monday morning quarter--back" or lay blame on anyone or anything, but it is important to learn from history, if at all possible, so to not have history repeat itself.

Darryl Kyle had an unusually strong history of heart disease in his family, with a father who died of a heart attack at an early age. Heart disease doesn't occur overnight. Atherosclerosis or hardening of the coronary arteries starts many years before it presents itself clinically, that is, before it presents itself by causing a heart attack.

If you knew that you had a strong family history of breast cancer or colon cancer, for instance, in a parent who had that disease at age 40, would you start getting mammograms or colonoscopy on yourself at age 40? No, you wouldn't, because even if you don't have medical training, it is intuitive that you should start looking for the disease to develop at an earlier age. You would probably get a mammogram in your twenties, since they are easy to do, and a colonoscopy you would reluctantly agree to (since it is more involved and uncomfortable) in your early thirties, if not sooner. You would do it even if you had no symptoms. You would hope that the cancer would be picked up at such an early stage that you could be on medications to cure it or prevent it from spreading so you could live a normal life span. And if your test was normal, you would have peace of mind. And you would probably repeat the test in a reasonable amount of time, say, five years.

Even without medical training, it would be reasonable for most people to think the test should be repeated in the future. Hopefully, you are able to balance the testing so you're not tested too frequently, so as not to add unnecessary costs to health care or additional inconvenience to yourself, but you would have the test repeated soon enough to pick up any early disease.

There is absolutely no doubt in my mind that an EBCT scan would have detected severe plaque in his coronary arteries, even if it was performed three or four years prior to his death! This is not an indictment of improper care by any means. But we need to think in terms of screening for coronary disease much like we screen for cancer.

The intent of this book is that we must get the message out that we do have a means to prevent cardiac death. Will we prevent all deaths? Of course not! Will a patient have a normal scan and still possibly die of a heart attack? That is possible because if the patient is having classical heart symptoms, a normal scan *does not* exclude the probability, because it may be soft plaque. But for this person, an invasive or noninvasive angiogram is needed. However, *for the person without symptoms, a normal scan means a very low chance of a heart attack.*

After Darryl Kyle died, I kept wondering why a professional sports team, which has millions of dollars invested in its athletes, wouldn't spend $500 to protect its investment? If not to protect its investment, then to protect a father and a husband from a disease to which he had a high likelihood of inheriting. If an athlete had a history of orthopedic injuries, a professional sports team would surely check the athlete for potential orthopedic problems. Why not evaluate professional athletes for heart related problems? I thought I already knew the answer, but I wanted to confirm my suspicions.

I knew that the failure to screen for heart disease couldn't be due to cost of testing. That just doesn't make sense. The cost of an EBCT scan is infinitesimal compared to the salaries. Living in Southern California, we are near many sports teams. Right after Darryl Kyle's death I called around to speak to some of the team trainers or the team physicians of a number of our different professional sports teams. I discussed with them the value of the scan, the simplicity of the test, the safety of the test, the inexpensive cost, and the availability and easy accessibility of the test. I also explained that I had scanned and worked with many other athletes and detected unexpected plaque in a large percentage of them.

I will never forget the answer I received from the athletic director of one of the teams, who shall remain unnamed. He said, "My guys do not need stress tests or scans; they are running up and down the court four hours a day without stopping—that is their stress test!"

I knew then that he did not understand one word I had been trying to tell him, not one word! He just didn't get the concept that you need to detect disease before it causes symptoms.

We had just discussed that Darryl Kyle also was able to perform as a professional athlete up to the day of his death. We discussed that he too also worked out, that he too also had a "daily stress test", so to speak.

Physical conditioning programs for most professional ball players are physically demanding. The fact that a player can participate in exercise without symptoms, does not mean the player is without risk for heart disease..

I asked Dick Butkus about the care professional athletes get, at least in his era. He explains it better in his own words, but in brief, it is not what it should be. Remember, Dick was 57 years old and had never even had a stress test. I truly believe that it is not because the teams don't care about the players, or that preventive care is too expensive. I think it is a mindset, in part born of ignorance about the value of testing.

Part of the mindset is that professional athletes compete at such a high level of performance, that it is human nature to believe that they are some how immune to the disease that will kill half of the rest of the population of the United States—heart disease! How can superb physically gifted people possibly compete as they do if they have heart disease! The other part of the problem is that there are still superb doctors in the general medical community who do not understand the value of the EBCT heart scans.

Another way to look at it is this: if you were to buy a used car that was a model known to have transmission trouble at 40,000 miles, and the one you were looking at to buy had 30,000 miles, would you have it checked out for transmission trouble before you buy it? If it did have a problem, you might still buy the car if they offered a discount, but you would have the choice to fix it before a mechanical disaster occurred.

Why then don't we do it with heart disease? The mindset has to change. You can't wait until you have symptoms. You need to detect heart disease early, before the symptoms arise.

People often will come for a treadmill stress test because they have a family history of heart disease, even if they have no symptoms. That is a good idea, because it will tell you if you have *advanced heart disease*, that is, coronary artery blockages that are so severe that those blockages are restricting blood flow. When a stress test is abnormal, the blockages have narrowed the arteries at least 70% or more. This means the disease is advanced.

Most often an intra-coronary stent or bypass surgery will be needed to open a severe restriction, *plus* the addition of medications to prevent the disease from progressing in the other arteries. Wouldn't it be better, safer, and less expensive to discover the disease before the stress test is abnormal so medications could prevent the need for surgery? We also know, as mentioned earlier, that most heart attacks occur from plaque that is not severe enough to narrow the coronary arteries, so there are no symptoms. Then the plaque ruptures, totally blocking blood flow and causing a heart attack. Wouldn't it be nice if we had a tool to detect the plaque early? We do have the tool and we have the means with the EBCT heart scan to detect it, and the guidelines in *The OC Heart Diet* to treat it properly!

What about John Ritter? Another talented celebrity in the prime of his career, another father and husband, John Ritter died of an aneurysm of the ascending aorta. The aorta is the largest blood vessel that leads out of the heart. An aneurysm means that the walls of the blood vessel (in this case, the aorta) have thinned out and expanded and dilated. Often, when the aorta expands to a certain size, there is a high probability of it rupturing (and causing almost certain death).

If the aneurysm is detected early enough, it can be surgically repaired and the person can return to a normal life. The autopsy findings are less clear for Mr. Ritter, but an EBCT scan of the heart also detects aneurysms of the ascending and thoracic aorta. It is not as certain in his case if an EBCT scan would have detected an aneurysm if it was done two or three years earlier. The point is, EBCT scans will often pick up other types of cardiovascular disease in one simple test.

What of the death of Bobby Hatfield? From all accounts there was no preceding history of heart disease or symptoms, yet as is commonly the case, sudden cardiac death is the first presentation of heart disease. I am quite sure an EBCT scan would have detected advanced plaque that most likely could have been treated med-ically or surgically.

I mention these three celebrities to bring to light the unnecessary loss of life in people of all walks of life, in the prime of their careers. I mention them because they are in the public eye. Every-day another well-known person is lost to the world, and their deaths should be a wakeup call to us all.

There is a way to prevent sudden death and heart attacks, obviously not for everyone, but at least there is a method to detect and treat people in a manner that provides *the best chance* to prolong life and also the quality of life. It is interesting that many people say, especially smokers, whom I council about the health risks of smoking, that they would prefer to continue smoking since it is so pleasurable to them. They often say that they don't care if they die in their sleep of a heart attack. I must remind them that they don't always have the choice to die peacefully in their sleep.

Many people have heart attacks and live, but the damage to their heart muscle is extensive enough that the pumping action of the heart is so diminished that they develop congestive heart failure. They live, but they live a very poor quality of life. They are unable to exercise due to weakness and shortness of breath. Often at night they cannot lie down because they can't breath. They require numerous medications to keep them functioning at the most simple tasks of daily living. They have innumerable admissions to the hospital for severe shortness of breath, requiring numerous testing procedures and blood tests. All in all, congestive heart failure can be a very unpleasant existence.

Blocked coronary arteries that lead to heart attacks are the main cause of congestive heart failure. Whatever the cause—tobacco abuse, high cholesterol, and so on—the point is EBCT scans detect plaque that can be treated to prevent ALL the consequences of coronary artery disease, whether it is sudden cardiac death, congestive heart failure, or chronic angina (chest pain).

5

What Is Heart Disease?

If you ask most people, "What is heart disease?" they will gen erally mention heart attacks as a definition of heart disease and that is the extent of it. For all practical purposes, coronary disease which leads to heart attacks accounts for over 90% of heart disease. The focus of *The OC Heart Diet* is about coronary artery disease, which accounts for almost half of all deaths in this country. However, for completeness, a brief understanding of the other forms of heart disease is in order, because *The OC Heart Diet* and the EBCT scan will not be helpful in detecting and treating these other forms of heart disease.

This is important to know and understand because if you have a history or family history of these forms of heart disease, there are other tests, other than the EBCT scan, that are better suited to detecting and treating these types of problems. A basic discussion of heart function and disease follows.

The heart is basically a ball of muscle about the size of your fist located slightly to the mid portion of the breastbone (sternum). The heart has four chambers: two small ones on the top, called atria, which simultaneously contract and pump blood across two small valves (which act as one-way doors), the tricuspid valve on the right side and the mitral valve on the left side. The two bottom chambers, the ventricles, receive the blood and then contract in unison; the right ventricle pumps old blood to the lungs to receive oxygen, the left ventricle receives new blood from the lungs, now full of oxygen. (See Figures on page 41.)

The left ventricle then pumps blood across the aortic valve into the major artery of the body, the aorta, which carries blood to the head, arms, and down to the abdomen and the rest of the body. For most purposes, when we talk about heart attacks, damage to the heart, or a weakened heart, we are talking about the left ventricle, which is the most important pumping chamber of the heart. If the left ventricle is damaged, we can't exercise because we can't pump adequate blood to our muscles. Likewise, we can't breathe because the weakened left ventricle can't pump blood out of our lungs.

Even though the heart chamber (the left ventricle) is constantly filled with blood, the heart muscle still needs its own blood supply in the form of the coronary arteries, which are on the surface of the heart and receive oxygen-rich blood from the aorta. It is these arteries that, when blocked, cause the most common form of heart disease—coronary artery disease.

There are three major coronary arteries: the right coronary supplies the bottom of the heart; the left main coronary artery divides into the left anterior descending artery, which supplies the front of the heart; and the circumflex artery, which supplies the back of the heart.

Each of these three major coronary arteries may have branch arteries that vary in size within any one individual. In general, the artery in the front, the left anterior descending, is the most important since it supplies the front of the heart, which does more of the pumping function than say the artery in the back of the heart. For this reason, a heart attack over the front of the heart is usually more serious than one in the back of the heart, because more of the pumping function of the heart is lost.

Another important aspect of the coronary arteries is the ability of the heart to develop small new interconnecting branches between the major arteries on the surface of the heart. These are called *collateral arteries*. The ability of one's body to develop collateral arteries is probably somewhat genetically determined; that is, some people develop a large number of collateral arteries, and some develop a few. It is clear that exercise helps promote the development of these collaterals.

The number of collaterals that one develops is important in determining how you may survive a heart attack. If the artery in the front starts to gradually close over time, for instance, in days to months your heart will sense the loss of adequate blood flow and start to develop collaterals from the right coronary artery.

The day of the heart attack, when the artery in the front totally closes, the collaterals from the right will, if of adequate size, provide blood flow to the area in the front that is deprived of normal blood flow and minimize the amount of damage that might otherwise occur. Collaterals are very important.

The heart valves work in unison to allow blood to flow in one direction from one heart chamber to the next. Heart valves can be defective from birth or can be damaged from infection or just wear and tear from the aging process. The valve can be narrowed and restrict the forward flow of blood through the heart chambers, or the valve can be leaky.

A leaky heart valve allows the blood flow to go in the reverse direction, which can lead to increased work for the heart chamber, and possible heart failure. Valvular heart disease is far less common than coronary artery disease. Though calcification of the heart valve can be seen on the EBCT scan, valvular heart disease is best assessed by an echocardiogram.

Finally, the last component of the heart structure is the sac around the heart called the *pericardium*. This is similar to the sac which surrounds the lungs, called the pleura. Most people are aware of pleurisy, which is a painful inflammation of the sac around the lungs. Similarly, there can be inflammation of the sac around the heart called *pericarditis,* which can also cause a sharp type of chest pain.

Of the above structures mentioned, the heart muscle, the heart valves, and the pericardium, there is another other diagnostic test which is preferred to image these structures. This test is the echocardiogram. The EBCT scan, for the purpose of *The OC Heart Diet*, is what is needed to see the plaque in the coronary arteries. The echocardiogram is preferred to evaluate heart valve disease.

The heart is a unique organ because it is constantly moving, constantly contracting. No other organ is in constant motion! This constant movement is what makes all tests that involve the heart somewhat more difficult to perform and analyze say than a simple x ray of the lungs to look for pneumonia, or an ultrasound of the kidneys or gallbladder to look for stones (gallstones or kidney stones). The gallbladder and kidneys are stationary. The heart, thankfully, is not.

Making it even more difficult to assess the heart is that each of the structures of the heart has not only a certain form but also a special function. Thus, the need for so many different tests since one test may show the structural details of the heart, and another test will show the function, eg blood flow. Some tests may seem redundant to a patient; after all, they are all "heart tests," but each provides unique information (though some tests provide overlapping information).

Other Tests for Heart Disease

Echocardiogram:- The echocardiogram is the most common heart test ordered after an electrocardiogram (EKG). The echocardiogram is the preferred test to determine *heart muscle function*, problems with the *sac around the heart* (pericardium), or *heart valve problems* (like mitral valve prolapse, narrowed or leaky heart valves, and the evaluation of heart murmurs).

The present echocardiograms are similar to but more sophisticated than other ultrasound tests that are used during pregnancy or for gallstones. The ultrasound waves are just as safe, but the heart is moving; hence, collecting the images is more complex and interpreting the images is also more complex, because not only are the structures of the heart being recorded but also the function.

Heart muscle function, that is, the ability to contract and pump blood, is best determined by the ultrasound test called the echocardiogram. Disease of the heart muscle is referred to as *cardiomyopathy,* which usually is due to prior heart attacks, but it also can be due to viral illnesses, excess alcohol, the effects of pregnancy, advanced disease of the heart valves, longstanding high blood pressure, and some congenital cardiomyopathies. Other tests that give information about the heart-muscle function are nuclear stress test as well as invasive and noninvasive angiograms, which require the injection of a dye.

The consequences of weakened heart muscle are two-fold:
- *Congestive heart failure* as discussed earlier.
- *Sudden cardiac death* due to a lethal arrhythmia.

A common measure of the heart function is the *ejection fraction,* which describes how much of the blood in the heart chamber is pumped out (ejected) with each contraction. A normal ejection fraction is 50%. A severely reduced ejection fraction is 35% or less. If you want to know about the pumping function of your heart (essentially, how strong your heart is), a resting echocardiogram is the simplest and arguably the best test to do.

Stress Testing: Stress testing is a means to detect a restriction of blood flow to the heart. This is an important distinction between EBCT scans and stress tests. EBCT scans tell you how much plaque (calcium) you have, and since the quantity of plaque correlates with the risk of a heart attack, the EBCT scan predicts your risk of a heart attack and how vigorously your risks need to be modified. The EBCT scan does not tell you if the plaque is restricting blood flow, though, in general, the larger the quantity of calcium, the more likely there is a restriction of blood flow.

Remember, most heart attacks occur because plaque in the lining of the coronary artery ruptures and abruptly closes off the

The stress test, on the other hand, measures *restriction of blood flow* in the coronary artery. So stress tests pick up *advanced* coronary artery disease. Disease that is severe enough to narrow the artery 70% or more will usually be detected 90% of the time. (That is, the stress test is 90% accurate in detecting blocked arteries.) The stress test will be "normal" even if there is extensive plaque as long as none of the plaque is narrowing the artery opening by more than 70%.

There are various types of stress tests. The simplest requires walking on a treadmill or riding a stationary bicycle and using a simple EKG. The EKG will show abnormalities as the heart rate increases if there is a restriction of blood flow. This type of stress

A more sophisticated stress test uses an accompanying echocardiogram, which will show that, as the heart rate increases, the walls of the heart are not contracting normally if there is a insufficient blood flow. This type of stress test is called a stress echocardiograms. Other tests require the injection of a radioactive dye into a vein during the exercise, then imaging the heart by lying on a table under a special nuclear camera. The radioactivity will not uniformly fill the heart if there is a restriction of blood flow. These are called nuclear stress tests and go by the name of Cardiolite, Myoview, or Thallium nuclear stress tests. Stress echocardiograms and nuclear stress tests are about 90% accurate in detecting a restriction of blood flow. If a stress test is abnormal, especially if there are accompanying symptoms, then the next test is usually an invasive coronary angiogram or a non-invasive CT angiogram.

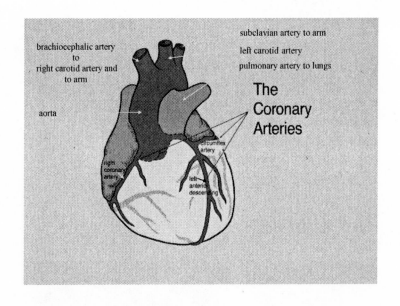

The Normal Heart

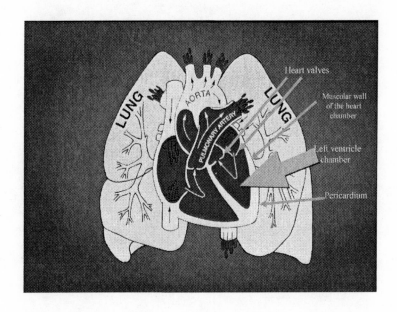

6

Which Heart Test Is For You?

To many patients, there appears to be a confusing array of heart tests available. Below is a simplified breakdown of which test may be appropriate for you.

EBCT Scan: For the Early Detection of Heart Disease
- If you are *without symptoms*
- If you have risk factors for heart disease

Stress Testing: To Detect Flow Restriction in Coronary Arteries

- If you *have symptoms* of chest discomfort or shortness of breath
- If you have an EBCT heart scan with significant calcium

A word about women and heart disease

It is now well established that women are more likely to die of heart disease than from any other cause. In fact, despite the popular belief that heart disease is a man's disease, more women than men die of heart disease.

What makes detecting heart disease in women more complex is usually women tend not to have the typical crushing chest pain that men so often present with. The symptoms that women get are far more subtle. Often, it may just be breathlessness, or fatigue, or distress in the upper abdomen. Adding to the difficulty in making the diagnosis, stress tests seem to be less accurate in detecting coronary artery blockages in women than they are in men. It is not known why stress tests are less accurate in women, but they are. In addition, when women do present with heart disease, the disease is far more advanced and extensive than it is in men.

Presently, there is a national campaign to focus on heart disease in women. The EBCT scan, in my opinion, should be part of any screening program to detect heart disease in women. Women Heart Centers are being formed at most major medical centers in the country to bring awareness to what many consider a disease epidemic in women. Screening women with resting EKGs, though better that nothing, adds little to detecting heart disease in the asymptomatic women. Recent studies confirm that in women, like in men, detecting coronary calcium by CT scans is more accurate than Framingham Risk Factors in detecting coronary artery disease. Choose a Women Heart Center that offers EBCT screening. EBCT scans deliver the lowest and safest radiation dose.

EBCT heart scans for coronary calcification are the most accurate means to detect heart disease in women.

7

The EBCT Scan

What is an EBCT Scan?

The *EBCT* scan stands for *Electron Beam Computerized Tomography.* This is a special type of CT scan that takes pictures of the heart very rapidly. Actually, it is much faster than conventional CT scans. As mentioned earlier, the heart is a unique organ in our body because it is always moving.

If a photo camera is taking a picture of a moving object, for example, a runner, the picture will be blurred if a fast-enough shutter speed is not used. So it is with CT scans taking pictures of our constantly moving hearts. The conventional CT scan has a mechanical lens that moves around the heart. Since it is mechanical, there is a limit to how fast it can rotate around the heart.

To speed up the picture-taking ability, multiple mechanical lenses are now being grouped together in the newest mechanical CT scanners. The speed to take the scan is increased, but the sharpness of the picture is not. The conventional CT scan's radiation exposure is much higher than that of an EBCT scan.

The EBCT scan uses an electron beam that quickly sweeps

from underneath the body while the person is lying on the table, and the image is received in the tungsten ring that curves over the person. The ring is stationary and acts as the film for the camera. Since the beam comes from behind and is electronic, it can sweep very quickly, essentially "freezing" the image of the heart. In addition, the amount of radiation is very minimal. At present the EBCT scan is the only CT scan approved by the FDA for coronary calcium scans. The conventional CT scanners and the EBCT scanners look identical externally.

The EBCT scan, like conventional CT scans, is an excellent screening tool to pick up lung cancers, much better that a conventional chest x-ray. Both EBCT scan and the conventional CT have been used to perform "full body scans," which not only scan the heart and lungs but also the abdomen, to detect abdominal aortic aneurysm, gallstones, kidney stones, and cancers of the organs of the abdomen.

Many people opt for full-body scans since the cost and time are only slightly more than a heart scan. I believe that it is heart disease that will be the most likely cause for most deaths, so if a full body scan is desired, it would best be done with an EBCT scan since it is the best type of scanner at present to *screen people with no symptoms of heart disease.*

If your EBCT scans shows calcium in the coronary arteries, then you have heart disease! It's called coronary artery disease since coronary arteries normally do not have calcium (plaque). It means the same as atherosclerosis (hardening of the arteries) of the heart. Does it mean you are doomed? Are you going to die tomorrow? No, not at all. You have to think of it differently. You must think along the lines that you have a problem, but you detected the problem early enough (after all, you are still alive and have not had a heart attack), and there are plenty of treatments available (and not necessarily surgical treatments) that can be put into place that can reverse the disease, or slow its progression, or fix it in such a way that will allow you to live a normal, active, and productive life. So many people have a scan; then they and many of their doctors don't know what to do with the results. On discovering that they have plaque, patients often are depressed or get a sense of hopelessness.

You should never be left with a sense of hopelessness after you receive the results of your scan. That is a failure to educate the person about what to do with the results of the scan, whether it is normal, slightly abnormal, or severely abnormal. Every test in medicine—be it a blood test, x-ray, or whatever—should be done with one thing in mind. Based on the results of that test, a certain action needs to be taken, or based on the test results, no action or intervention needs to be taken.

A normal test is as valuable as an abnormal test. A normal test of any kind gives peace of mind and allows you to look for other causes of a symptom or allows you to relax, knowing no serious problem will occur and you can go about your normal life. It is not uncommon for a patient to have a very abnormal stress test, then need to go on to have an invasive angiogram (heart catheterization and coronary angiogram) to see if the abnormalities on the treadmill really represent critically blocked coronary arteries.

Perhaps 10% of the time the invasive angiogram will be normal—not show any severe blockages. This means the stress test was a false positive. It indicated a blockage—that is, it was "positive" or "abnormal" (negative test results mean it is normal) — yet the angiogram, being the gold standard or reference test, was normal.

Patients will often say that since the angiogram was normal, that they really didn't need the angiogram in the first place. They become upset having to have a test that was normal. That is exactly the wrong way of thinking. They should think that they now have a conclusively normal test, and they can get back to a normal life.

Remember, they had a 90% chance of the angiogram being abnormal, with all the implications that can go with it, like the need for an intra-coronary stent or the need for coronary bypass surgery. My point is that a normal test is as valuable as an abnormal test. Whether it is a blood test for thyroid problems, an EBCT scan of your heart, or a gallbladder ultrasound, the key issue is what to do with the information! The education of the patient is *critical in making the EBCT scan a successful tool in saving lives!*

I strongly believe that no one should have an EBCT scan with the results being reported as yes, there is calcium or no, there is no calcium. If there is calcium, the person needs to be educated about lifestyle changes; and, if needed, other tests may need to be done, as well as cholesterol treatment guidelines based on the score for that person. Recommendations for when a repeat scan should be done can then be given. There is plenty of scientific data available on EBCT scans upon which to make these recommendations.

How is the EBCT Scan performed?

Keep in mind that the EBCT scan is a very quick and painless test to take. You lie on a table fully clothed, you hold your breath for less than thirty seconds, and the scanner takes pictures of your heart and lungs. There is no special preparation or intravenous lines or needles required for the test. The table moves through a large ring or tube. The tube is quite large and not at all claustrophobic like an MRI scan.

In another minute, without the need to hold your breath, the scan of the abdomen is complete. Total time on the table for a full-body scan is less than ten minutes. The scan of only the heart and lungs takes less than five minutes. The scan is so quick and simple to take that the significance of the test is lost on most patients unless it is carefully reviewed with the patient.

The EBCT scan findings should be discussed and the significance of the findings explained to the patient immediately after the scan is performed. It is not enough to tell a patient that he or she has calcium or plaque in the arteries and leave it at that. The scan is wasted unless a plan or recommendation is given based on the results. A medical practitioner should review the results of the scan with you; then a typewritten report should be sent to you after the heart scan is finally reviewed by a cardiologist, and the lungs and abdomen are reviewed by a radiologist. Recommendations are included with the final report.

There are other important considerations at the time of EBCT scan: a brief medical history should be taken to see if there are any symptoms or past medical problems. It is extremely important to find out if any suspected cardiac symptoms are present. *Rarely a patient may have soft, non-calcified plaque that will not show up on the EBCT scan that could be obstructing blood flow. The person who is having symptoms needs further testing under the care of a physician.*

Who should have an EBCT Scan?

For any type of medical test there are guidelines for performing the tests. A mammogram, colonoscopy, or cholesterol screening are recommended based on guidelines founded on medical data about the disease that you are trying to screen for.

The goal is to screen as many people as possible so as not to miss anyone that is likely to have the disease, balancing that against not performing tests on people who are unlikely to have the disease. In other words, you don't want to unnecessarily test someone, since there is expense associated with all tests, perhaps some risk and perhaps some discomfort. Yet you don't want to miss anyone, either. But guidelines are just that, a recommendation based on a general population of people.

There are many people who fall out of the guidelines for any test. That is, though they maybe older or younger than the usual age range for the test, a circumstance may arise where early testing is reasonable. For instance, a family prone to breast cancer in their early twenties may want to screen members in their late teenage years. So it is with EBCT scans; the guidelines for EBCT heart scans are not absolute.

The following guidelines are not all inclusive, but they are reasonable for people who self-refer themselves for a test. The reason why it is important to have guidelines is because a vast majority of the scans are done at the direct request of the patient. Under these circumstances the recommendations should be more restrictive so patients do not take a test that would be of little benefit for them. A physician, with an expected more comprehensive knowledge base, may want to order a test for reasons that are more encompassing than the guidelines indicate.

Guidelines for EBCT Heart Scanning

A man older than 35, or a woman older than 40, with at least one of the following risk factors should receive the scan:

- **High total cholesterol**
  If no coronary calcium is present, the cholesterol medications can be avoided and diet and exercise can be tried.

- **Low HDL (low good cholesterol) and normal total cholesterol**
  If there is coronary calcium, then niacin or a fibrate should be used to raise the low HDL, even if the total cholesterol is normal.

- **Family history of heart disease**
  Even if the cholesterol is normal, if there is coronary calcification, then cholesterol medications would be beneficial.

- **High blood pressure**
  Even if the cholesterol is normal, if there is coronary calcium, then cholesterol medications would be beneficial.

- **Tobacco use**
  If coronary calcium is present, cholesterol medications would be beneficial. In addition, you should have a lung scan at the same time, since the EBCT scan of the lungs is the best test to detect lung cancer. The lung scan will only take one minute more than the heart scan alone.

- **Obesity**
  If coronary calcium is present, cholesterol medications would be beneficial even if the cholesterol is normal.

Recommendations based on the EBCT scan results

The following recommendations are made:
- **The need for stress testing**
  If there is a significant amount of calcium on the scan, a stress test should be done to see if the plaque is restricting blood flow. The more plaque present, the more likely there may be a restriction of blood flow.

- **The levels of cholesterol control**
  The higher the calcium score for your age and gender, the more vigorously your cholesterol needs to be treated. For instance, the calcium score helps determine the cholesterol goal: should the LDL (bad cholesterol) be reduced to 160, or 130, or 100?

- **The interval when the EBCT scan should be repeated**
  The EBCT scan should be repeated in eighteen to twenty-four months if there is calcium; otherwise, you will not know if the course of treatment has been effective. Often, if the treatment is correct, the plaque may regress somewhat. If the plaque progresses, that is a sign that even more vigorous medication and diet changes are needed. If there is no calcium, usually the scan can be repeated in four to five years. It is usually not necessary to repeat the scan sooner than eighteen months.

- **Diet and exercise recommendations should be given**
  The OC Heart Diet program will fill the needs even if there is no calcium present.

As you can see from the above recommendations, the scan will help to decide if medical treatment needs to be administered. Depending on the amount of calcium, starting a cholesterol medication could be life saving. If no calcium is present, you can possibly avoid the cost and inconvenience of taking a cholesterol medication.

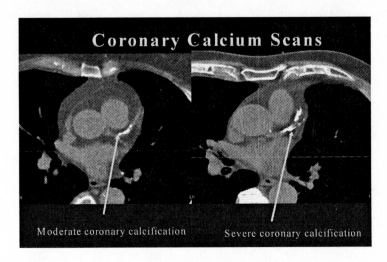

Coronary calcification

Should You Have a Lung or Full-body Scan?

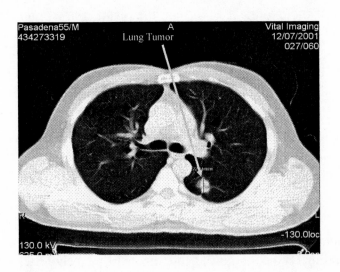

Lung Scan

Lung Scan

If you are a smoker, you should definitely have a lung scan when you have your heart scan. The cost increase is probably less than $200. The radiation dose is minimal, and the time to take the scan is only one to two minutes more.

Full-body Scan

The full-body scan takes an additional five minutes when added to the heart and lung scan and adds another $150 to $200 dollars to the cost. The full-body can pick up aortic aneurysms, cancers of the liver and kidneys, kidney stones, gallbladder stones, osteoporosis, prostate enlargement, and other conditions. Bone density is measured as part of a full-body scan. The radiation dose obviously goes up. Serious problems often are detected, but the yield is less than for a heart scan simply because there is more disease in the heart than diseases in other organs of the body.

Virtual Colonoscopy
See Graphic Following Page

This is a new type of colonoscopy performed by filling the colon with air and then scanning the abdomen with the EBCT scan. Preparation for the test is similar to a traditional colonoscopy; however, the virtual colonoscopy requires no sedation. It is more comfortable and quicker to perform than a traditional colonoscopy

Who should *not* have an EBCT Heart Scan?

There is no absolute reason not to have an EBCT scan. However, there are some situations where another test, or at least physician guidance, is needed before having the scan:

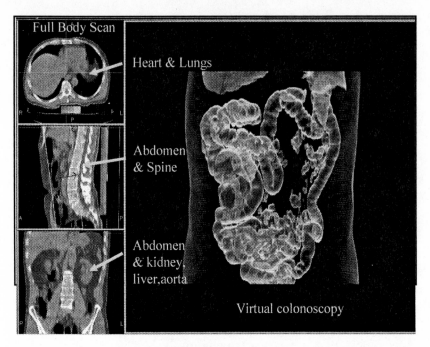

Virtual Colonoscopy

• If you are having symptoms

If you are having symptoms such as chest pain or chest tightness, shortness of breath, or passing out, you need to see a doctor first before having the EBCT heart scan. Even though the scan can be very helpful to a person having symptoms that may be heart related, the issues become more complex and should be under the guidance of a doctor. For instance, if you are having chest pain that occurs with exertion, there is a very high probability that it is angina (chest pain due to a narrowed coronary artery). The EBCT may be very helpful, but your physician may decide that a stress test or an invasive coronary angiogram (heart catheterization) or a noninvasive angiogram (EBCT scan with the injection of a dye into the vein) may be a more important test to do.

• If you have a prior history of heart disease

The EBCT scan test will surely show calcification on your coronary arteries if you have already had a heart attack or an intra-coronary stent or coronary bypass surgery. It is not that the test is without value in these situations; it is helpful in repeating the test over the years to see if the diet and cholesterol treatment are preventing plaque formation. However, since you know heart disease is present, we already know how vigorously we need to control diet and cholesterol, based on present guidelines.

However, if the subsequent test two years later shows significantly more calcium, then even lower cholesterol levels will be required. The EBCT scan alone will also not tell you if the stent or coronary bypass grafts are still open. You would need to inject dye at the time of the EBCT scan (noninvasive angiogram) to see if the stent or grafts are open. A noninvasive angiogram (also called a CT angiogram) should be done under the direction of your doctor.

What are the arguments made against an EBCT Scan?

Every medical test seems to have physicians who are proponents for the test and those physicians who are against performing the test. This is especially true when a test is relatively new like an EBCT calcium scan. As time goes on, the benefits and utility of the test become better known and more widely accepted. The following are some of the arguments made against the EBCT scan, and what I feel are the arguments in favor of the scan:

• **The EBCT scan is too expensive!**

The truth is the test is relatively inexpensive for the information provided. The heart-only scan costs about $350 to $400. If you have no calcium, you can potentially avoid cholesterol medications for several years, even if your cholesterol is elevated, and you can work with diet and exercise. A four-month supply of a cholesterol medicine like Lipitor is about $350.

• **The radiation dose is too high.**

The truth is that the radiation dose from an EBCT heart scan is very low, about the equivalent of two to three routine chest x-rays. It is less than the average amount of radiation that a person gets from the atmosphere when living at high elevations like Denver, Colorado, for three months.

A recent article sensationalized the effects of the radiation dose from full-body scans. The article said (to paraphrase) that the radiation dose was similar to that received by survivors of the atomic bomb. They theorized that it will lead to an increase in cancer rates if full-body-scan use becomes more widespread for screening purposes.

What they did not say was that the radiation doses that they were talking about were only from conventional or multislice CT scans. *EBCT scans have five to ten times less radiation than a conventional CT scan, and only EBCT scans should be used for heart, lung, or full-body screening because of their very low radiation.* In addition, the x-ray beam from the EBCT scan comes from underneath the body (through the back when you are supine on the table), therefore exposing breast tissue (in particular) to very, very low doses of radiation.

• **Everyone has calcium, and it doesn't mean you have blockages.**

Everyone doesn't have coronary calcium. If you have calcium, you may not have a significantly blocked artery, but the amount of calcium present is *the best predictor* of your future chance of having a coronary event, or needing coronary stents or bypass surgery. When coronary calcium is found early enough, you can be medically treated and possibly prevent a coronary event.

• **The EBCT scan picks up insignificant abnormalities that lead to unnecessary testing.**

If you have coronary calcium, you have coronary artery disease, period! There are no "false positive" tests. If you have calcium, you have plaque. If you have plaque, you will need treatment of some sort and future monitoring.

What do we do with the results?

Three numbers are reported based on the quantity of coronary calcium: total calcium score, calcium volume, and calcium percentile.

• **Calcium score**

This represents all the combined calcium in all of the three major coronary arteries, as well as in the major branch arteries.
Studies have shown that the higher the calcium score, the higher the chance you will have a coronary event (an event is described as a heart attack, sudden cardiac death, or the need for coronary bypass surgery or a coronary stent). This is because the more calcium you have, the more extensive the atherosclerosis.
Between all the pieces of calcium are soft, non-calcified plaque. The more calcified plaque, the more soft non-calcified plaque. Soft plaque is not seen with the scan. It is the soft plaque that suddenly develops a tear or "ruptures" and causes a heart attack. The calcified plaque generally causes gradual closure that leads to the gradual onset of angina, which needs to be controlled with medications, stents, or coronary bypass surgery.
Therefore, the higher the score, the more vigorously the cholesterol needs to be controlled to prevent cardiac events. The higher the score, the more likely the calcified plaque may be obstructing blood flow, so a stress test is recommended to detect the obstruction of blood flow. If the subsequent stress test is abnormal, then at the discretion of the cardiologist, a coronary angiogram may be recommended.

• Calcium volume

The computer derives a volume of plaque based on a formula that takes into account the calcium score and how dense the plaque is. Calcium volume is the best indicator to follow to see if plaque is growing. If plaque is left untreated, it can increase in volume sometimes up to 50% per year. It seems that a volume increase of 10% or less per year is safe. When the volume increases by more than 20% per year then the plaque is active and risk of a possible cardiac event increases. More vigorous cholesterol control is then warranted. It is important to repeat the EBCT calcium scan (if the score is above zero) every 18 to 24 months to see if the medical treatment regimen is effective.

• Calcium percentile

The percentile represents how you score compared to other persons of your age and gender. The reason the percentile is important is that it gives you an idea of how aggressive you athero-sclerosis is. If you are a woman 40 years of age with a total calcium score of 25, this would place you in the 95th percentile, which means you have more plaque than 95% of other women your age. Please note that it does *not* mean that you have an artery that is 95% blocked! That is the most common misperception about the results.

Also notice that in the above example, though the total score is not very high, it is very high for that age. The plaque can some-times double each year if left untreated. So, by the age of 60, the chance that you would have a coronary event would be extremely high if you did not institute vigorous cholesterol treatment when you were in your forties. A total calcium score of 25 in a sixty-year-old woman places you in the less than fiftieth percentile. You still need treatment, but it can be less aggressive and still prevent cardiac events.

Calcium Score Percentiles

6,683 Males—Asymptomatic
Male Calcium Score Percentiles

Age	25th	50th	75th	90th	96th
30–34	0	0	0	1	2
35–39	0	0	0	8	55
40–44	0	0	4	62	135
45–49	0	0	32	174	295
50–54	0	8	83	319	505
55–59	1	50	229	665	1172
60–64	7	100	440	1145	1548
65–69	39	232	705	1522	2382
70–74	88	336	929	2443	3296

Friede 1999

Calcium Score Percentiles

4,004 Females—Asymptomatic
Female Calcium Score Percentiles

Age	25th	50th	75th	90th	96th
30–34	0	0	0	0	0
35–39	0	0	0	0	1
40–44	0	0	0	0	3
45–49	0	0	0	4	28
50–54	0	0	0	29	67
55–59	0	0	6	82	182
60–64	0	0	31	175	375
65–69	0	13	111	332	817
70–74	0	18	211	522	884

Friede 1999

An additional usefulness of the percentile is that it gives an idea if there may be other factors contributing to plaque formation. These other factors are referred to in the advanced lipid panel that is described below.

In Summary

Based on the *total calcium score* and the *calcium percentile,* these recommendations are made:

- The cholesterol goals needed to achieve regression or stabilization of plaque to prevent future cardiac events.
- The need for a stress test (assuming there are no symptoms)
- A reasonable time to do a follow-up scan
- The need to do an advanced lipid profile to look for other causes of plaque.
- The need for aspirin. Anyone with plaque would benefit from aspirin (unless there is a contraindication like stomach ulcers or aspirin allergy).
- The need for cholesterol-lowering drugs as well as the type of cholesterol-lowering drugs. The types of drugs (that is, a statin, fibrate, niacin, or others) are based on the advanced lipid profile results discussed later.

Cholesterol Goals

<u>No coronary calcium</u>:
LDL < 160
HDL > 40
Triglycerides < 200
No stress test needed unless symptoms
Repeat scan 5 years

Note: if you are a diabetic and have no coronary calcium, you should follow guidelines similar to those with calcium score of greater than 399.

<u>Ca Score 1–99 and ≤ 50th Percentile</u>
LDL < 130
HDL > 45
Triglycerides < 150
Daily ASA 81 mg
Repeat scan 2 years

<u>Ca Score 100–399 or > 50th Percentile</u>
LDL < 100
HDL > 45 to 50
Triglycerides < 150
Advanced Lipid Testing
Stress Testing
Daily ASA 81 mg
Repeat scan 2 years

<u>Ca Score >399 or > 75th Percentile</u>
LDL < 100, near 70
HDL > 45 to 50
Triglycerides < 100
Advanced Lipid Testing
Stress Testing
Daily ASA 81 mg
Repeat scan 2 years

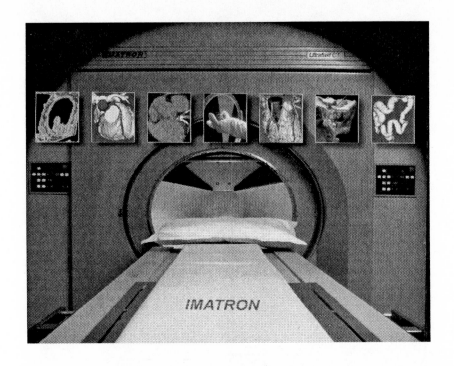

Schematic of Electron Beam CT Scanner

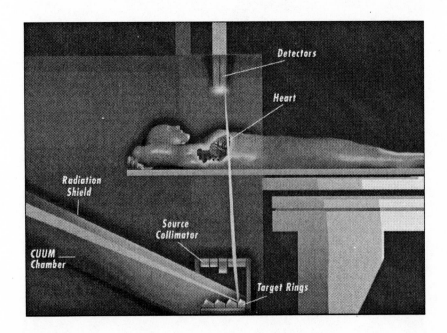

8

Sample EBCT Report

OC Vital *Imaging*

Patient Name:	Examination Date:
Mr. John E. Doe **M (49)**	1/10/2006
Address:	
1111 Fifth Avenue	
Anytown, CA 90000	
Patient Physician:	Susan Doe, MD

TECHNIQUE:

The patient underwent high-resolution, volume-mode, axial Electron Beam Tomography (with 3-millimeter slices at 2-millimeter table increments) of the heart obtained at 100 millisecond scan times, in conjunction with ECG-gating at mid diastole. The matrix size of 512 x 512 with a 26-centimeter FOV (field of view) was used, giving a pixel size of $0.258mm^2$ with a $0.774mm^3$ volume.

HISTORY:

The patient's lipids are elevated. Lipids are currently untreated. There is a family history of heart disease, stroke, and diabetes. Chest pain with exertion has

John Doe
January 10, 2006
Page 2

been reported in the past. The patient currently reports unusual fatigue. A previous stress echocardiogram performed in 2003 was normal. The patient uses daily aspirin. The patient is treated for hypertension. The patient is an occasional smoker. The patient has Type II diabetes mellitus that is treated with diet and exercise. The patient currently participates in an exercise regimen but not on a regular basis.

FINDINGS:

Location	# Lesions	Volume mm³	Calcium Score	Density
LM	1	56	60	1.2
LAD	3	228	259	1.1
CX	4	350	375	1.1
RCA	6	450	500	1.1
Total	14	1,084	1,194	1.1

Table 1

LM = left main coronary **LAD = left anterior descending artery**
CX = circumflex artery **RCA = right coronary artery**

HEART FINDINGS:
Calcified atherosclerotic plaque structure was identified in the coronary arteries as summarized in **Table 1** by: number of lesions, plaque volume, calcium scores, and density. The results are calculated by each major coronary artery. Risk is assessed by correlation of the total calcium score with a calcium score database based upon the Electron Beam CT scanner. The Density is a means to further assess the calcific deposits. A Density less than 1 indicates more dense average calcification. A Density greater than 1 represents less dense average calcification.

The patient shows a coronary artery calcification score of **1.194**. Moderately dense calcification is seen in the left main coronary artery. Moderately dense calcification is seen in the proximal and mid-left anterior descending coronary artery. Moderately dense calcification is seen scattered in the circumflex coronary artery. Moderately dense calcification is seen scattered throughout the right

John Doe
January 10, 2006
Page 3

coronary artery. There is moderate calcification in the ascending, descending aorta and aortic arch.

IMPRESSIONS and RECOMMENDATIONS:

Coronary artery calcification score of **1,194** consistent with a **very high** probability for the presence or future development of obstructive coronary artery disease in a patient in this age group. The score is greater than the 95th percentile for the patient's age group. Asymptomatic patients in this scoring/age range have about a 20% to 40% chance of current obstructive coronary artery disease, but left untreated, a 21-fold increased future risk of myocardial infarction when compared with patients who have no coronary artery calcification.

Recommendations Include:

1. All results should be reviewed with your personal physician. Consultation with the personal physician is recommended to evaluate symptoms of fatigue.

2. A current stress test or stress echocardiogram is recommended.

3. A current lipid panel is necessary for proper management. In addition to the calcium score, proper management will be based upon age, risk factors, and history. In this patient with substantial calcific plaque burden, secondary prevention guidelines are recommended. To most effectively slow or stop progression and reduce future risk, the following lipid goals are recommended: LDL cholesterol below 100mg/dl; HDL cholesterol near or above 50mg/dl; triglycerides below 150mg/dl and ideally near 100mg/dl.

4. Given the family history of heart disease and the substantial amount of coronary artery calcification for the patient's age, further testing for Lp(a) as well as LDL and HDL subclasses (Advanced Heart Panel) may be considered. It is possible that an inherited, atherogenic trait that is not apparent with conventional lipid testing is present. This is very important because it can provide the information necessary to establish the proper individualized treatment. Additional recommended laboratory studies as follow: high sensitivity CRP.

John Doe
January 10, 2006
Page 4

5. Due to the presence of calcified atherosclerotic plaque, a daily 81mg (baby) aspirin is recommended as a precaution to reduce thrombosis risk unless contraindicated.

6. Repeat scan in 2 years to assess plaque progression.

7. NOTE: Smoking cessation is important. The erosive effect of smoking on the endothelium along with the increased propensity for thrombus formation <u>increase the risk for sudden myocardial infarction and sudden death, even in patients with minimal atherosclerotic plaque development.</u>

8. Please be aware that reports of new studies performed to screen for lung cancer in smokers and former smokers 40 years of age or older have shown that nearly as many new cancers are found on the second or third year of follow-up as were found on the initial screening test. Therefore, to be most effective in screening for lung cancer, OC Vital Imaging strongly recommends that persons who smoke or <u>have smoked in the past</u> have the lung portion of the screening study repeated annually.

9. Exercise and weight control can be very beneficial to the heart by stabilizing atherosclerotic plaque, controlling blood pressure, lowering triglycerides, and raising HDL (good cholesterol). The minimum exercise for healthy people is 30 minutes, 3 to 4 times per week. Optimal exercise is 60 minutes, 6 to 7 times weekly. Any new or increased level of physical activity should have the approval of the personal physician prior to initiation.

10. A weight loss of 15 to 20 pounds is recommended.

11. The American Heart Association recommends avoiding trans-fatty acids and limiting saturated fat to less than 10% of energy. Substitute unsaturated fat and consume both whole grains and at least 5 servings of vegetables and fruits daily. The AHA also indicates that "foods rich in omega-3 polyunsaturated fatty acids, specifically EPA and DHA, confer cardioprotective effects. Food sources of omega-3 fatty acids include fish, especially fatty fish such as salmon, as well as plant sources such as flaxseed and flaxseed oil,

John Doe
January 10, 2006
Page 5

canola oil, soybean oil, and nuts. At least 2 servings of fish per week are recommended to confer cardioprotective effects." (From AHA Guidelines, Revision 2000)

12. Proper control of blood pressure lowers the risk of cardiovascular disease. A minimum target is below 140/90; a goal of less than 130/85 should be used for higher risk patients (e.g., known cardiovascular disease, diabetes, kidney disease, stroke, and peripheral vascular disease).

13. Optimal control of diabetes can reduce the risk of further atherosclerosis development.

Thank you, Mr. Doe, for the opportunity to provide this examination for you.

Orange County Heart Institute
Medical Director

gf
T: Tuesday, January 10, 2006

Radiology Report

Doe, John
DOB: 09/24/56
DOE: 09/11/05

Disclaimer: Noncontrast screening CT scans may be less sensitive than CT scans with intravenous contrast for evaluation of masses of the mediastinum, liver, spleen, kidneys, or pancreas, as well as evaluation of the blood vessels. CT is not sensitive for evaluation of the viscera (hollow organs) such as the stomach and bowel. A physician familiar with the patient's history and clinical condition should review the results. If the patient has symptoms or any known disease, additional studies may be necessary. The radiologist will not review or interpret images of the heart.

_____

John Smith, MD, Radiologist
Diplomate, American Board of Radiology

9

What Causes Heart Disease?

The traditional risk factors for heart disease—high blood pressure, diabetes, high cholesterol, and obesity—can all be improved with exercise and *The OC Heart Diet*. It is important to remember that multiple risk factors create a manifold increase in the risk for heart disease. If you have two risk factors, your risk of heart disease does not just double, it may increase eight fold. The recommendations for cholesterol levels based on the EBCT calcium score take into account any additional risk factors that may be present in a particular patient. As time goes on, new risk factors are discovered, and some of the emerging risk factors are discussed below. What is clear and so disturbing is that you can have none of the now known risk factors and develop heart disease, or have all of the known risk factors and not develop heart disease. The EBCT scan helps level the playing field because it tells you with high probability if you do or do not have heart disease.

What Causes Heart Disease?

Classic Factors Associated with Heart-disease Risk

These explain only 60% of heart disease:
- Age
- Male gender
- Family history
- High blood cholestero
- High blood pressure
- Diabetes
- Metabolic syndrome
- Obesity
- Sedentary lifestyle
- Tobacco abuse
- Unknown in at least 35 to 40%

About classic Framingham Risk Factors

Age

No doubt about it that your risk goes up with age. What is astounding is how early coronary disease can develop. At autopsy, fatty streaks (the earliest form of disease) can be seen in the lining of the coronary arteries as early as 20 years of age!

Male gender

Women tend to develop coronary disease 10 to 15 years later than men, probably due to the protective effect of their natural estrogen production. When estrogen levels drop during menopause, coronary disease becomes much more common in women, and indeed becomes the leading cause of death of women in the United States. Despite the controversy about hormone replacement therapy in women, estrogen replacement (without accompanying progesterone) slows the development of coronary disease, as seen by EBCT scanning, in postmenopausal women.

Family history

Obviously your genetic background explains a lot of disease patterns. Recent research has shown that heart disease in your sibling is a more important risk factor than heart disease in your parents. This probably reflects the influence of heredity *and* environment. That is, siblings tend to have similar eating habits etc. as they grown up which adds to their common genetic predisposition.

High blood pressure

High blood pressure is called the "silent killer" because it insidiously promotes coronary and other vascular disease without causing symptoms, until the damage is done. Our traditional definitions of high blood pressure are changing based on what other risk factors co-exist. The traditional recommendations are that the systolic pressure should be less than 140mm and the diastolic pressure should be less than 90mm. If there is accompanying diabetes, then a blood pressure of 135/85 or lower is recommended. It seems that there really is not a distinct cut off where risk begins and where no risk exists from blood pressure. Rather, the risk is linear. That is, a systolic blood pressure of 130 places you at slightly higher risk that a systolic pressure of 125. *The OC Heart Diet* will help those with high blood pressure to more readily control this silent killer.

Diabetes

The bad news is that diabetes is a growing epidemic and is a major risk factor for heart disease. The good news is that there is now substantial evidence that strict blood sugar control can slow or prevent the ravages of diabetes, whether it be Type 1 (also called juvenile diabetes or insulin dependant) or Type 2 (also called adult onset or non-insulin dependant diabetes). What is also clear is that the growing obesity problem in this country is a major contributor to the development of diabetes later in life. *The OC Heart Diet,* with the approval of your doctor, will greatly benefit the control of diabetes.

71

Metabolic Syndrome and Insulin Resistance

Metabolic syndrome is a close relative of full blown diabetes and is now considered a major risk factor for heart disease. In recent years it has become a major focus on the war against heart disease. Metabolic syndrome is a cluster of risk factors which may occur together and increase your risk for heart disease, diabetes, strokes and peripheral vascular disease. The underlying process seems to be insulin resistance. Insulin is a hormone excreted by the pancreas in response to the intake of sugars and carbohydrates. Insulin then promotes the update of glucose (blood sugar) into muscle cells and other organs. When insulin resistance occurs, the pancreas must secrete higher and higher levels of insulin to promote the cells to uptake glucose. The cells are essentially resistant or relatively incapable of responding to insulin. The higher circulating levels of insulin in the blood stream and the higher than normal levels of blood sugar lead to a host of reactions that cause inflammation of arteries and the subsequent formation of plaque in the arteries. Central body fat or visceral fat as discussed below in the section on obesity, seems to be a primary contributor to metabolic syndrome and insulin resistance.

Research into the complex underlying process linking this group of conditions is ongoing. In addition to now known factors as obesity, inactivity, excess alcohol and smoking, a recent British study suggests job stress is a contributing factor for metabolic syndrome. Fructose (sugar found in fruit, honey and corn syrup) has also been cited, in the latest research, as another contributing factor to metabolic syndrome.

The diet and exercise programs in *The OC Diet* are very effective in treating metabolic syndrome and insulin resistance.

Diagnosis of Metabolic Syndrome

According to present guidelines, you have metabolic syndrome
if you have three or more of these traits:

- **Central obesity (apple shaped body)**

   Waist circumference, greater than 35 inches for women
   and 40 inches for men. Another measure is waist to hip
   ratios: Men with waist-to-hip ratios greater than 0.95 or
   women with ratios above 0.8 are at increased risk.

- **High triglycerides**

   150 milligrams per deciliter (mg/dL) or higher, or you're
   receiving treatment for high triglycerides.

- **Low HDL**

   Less than 40 mg/dL in men or less than 50 mg/dL in
   women or you're receiving treatment for low HDL.

- **Blood pressure**

   130 millimeters of mercury (mm Hg) systolic (the top
   number) or higher or 85 (mm Hg) diastolic (the bottom
   number) or higher, or you're receiving treatment for
   high blood pressure.

- **High fasting blood sugar (blood glucose)**

   100 mg/dL or higher, or you're receiving treatment for
   high blood sugar.

A quick rule of thumb: If you have central obesity (apple shaped)
and a triglyceride/HDL ratio 3.5 or 4.0 to 1, there is high probability of metabolic syndrome. Thirty percent of middle age people in the United States are actually insulin resistant. Sixty percent of those with cardiovascular disease have insulin resistance.

Obesity

Any amount of *excess weight* increases your risk of heart disease even if you have normal blood pressure and cholesterol. Obesity is a growing epidemic in the United States. An estimated 30% of all Americans are considered obese, which means they have a body mass index more than 30 (see chapter 14 for more information about body mass index).

What is it about body fat that contributes to heart disease? Is all body fat the same? It turns out that not all body fat is the same. There is *subcutaneous body fat*, the kind that we have on our back, legs, arms, buttocks and under the skin over the abdomen. The second type fat is *visceral fat,* which is the type fat that is in the abdominal cavity, covering the intestines, liver and other organs, as well as the fat that covers the surface of the heart.

The observation has been made that in obese and moderately overweight people there are two body types based on fat distribution in the body. There is the "pear-shaped" and the "apple-shaped" body types. The pear shaped body is where the fat is mainly on the hips, buttocks and thighs. The pear-shaped body has the fat more in the subcutaneous areas and thus has proportionally less visceral body fat. Pear-shaped bodies have less risk for heart disease than those with "apple shaped" bodies. The apple-shaped body has more of the fat in the belly area. This is also referred to as "central obesity." The apple-shaped body is at higher risk for heart disease than the pear-shaped body. Of course, obesity of any body shape has higher risk for heart disease than the non-obese person. You can also have a high degree of visceral fat even if you are not overweight. This occurs especially in those who are very sedentary, and eat high saturated fat diets and excess alcohol.

Visceral fat is not just an inactive collection of fat globules, but a vast, interconnected organ that secretes and regulates hormones and numerous other substances. Visceral fat is an organ that has a huge effect on body metabolism and most other organs. Some of the substances secreted by visceral fat are adiponectin, leptin and cytokines. These substances along with numerous other compounds contribute to various functions including inflammation of the arteries, increase fat uptake by the liver with subsequent deposition in the arteries and resistance to insulin's action (referred to as *insulin resistance* discussed above) by the body. In other words, the more visceral fat you have, the higher the risk of heart disease. This is due to inflammation of the arteries, increase in diabetes, and an increase in triglycerides and a decrease in the HDL (good) cholesterol.

So how do you get rid of visceral fat? Exercise is crucial in getting rid of visceral fat, and not surprisingly, exercise is a mainstay in treating diabetes. It turns out that the exercise recommended in *The OC Heart Diet* is a very effective way treatment. That is, resistance training *and* aerobic exercise are more effective than aerobic exercise alone in reducing visceral fat. Interestingly, doing sit-ups and other abdominal exercises alone are not as effective in reducing central body fat as is all over body conditioning and aerobic exercise. Reducing saturated fat and excess alcohol is the second part of the equation.

Sedentary Lifestyle

Physical inactivity sets up a whole host of problems for your body. Muscle mass decreases, bone density decreases, visceral fat increases, and blood pressure tends to increase. In addition, HDL cholesterol tends to decrease, blood sugars and triglycerides tend to increase. Increasing activity even five minutes per day can substantially change your risk for heart disease. In short, exercise is one of the most effective and least expensive pills ever devised in preventing heart disease. Exercise is discussed in extensive detail in subsequent chapters.

Tobacco

Tobacco use requires special emphasis. The damaging effects of tobacco smoke on the vascular system are overwhelming. Especially dangerous is diabetes and smoking. Diabetics who smoke often have such extensive damage to the arteries of the heart, legs, and neck that when the patient does present with symptoms, surgical correction often is extremely difficult, with poor surgical outcomes and a low rate of long-term success.

Of all the corrective measures to take to prevent heart disease, quitting smoking is the most crucial. It is important to remember that the nicotine is not particularly harmful, other than it is addicting. Nicotine does not directly cause plaque formation. It is the hundreds of harmful products in the tobacco smoke that cause hardening of the arteries. In addition, these products cause spasm of the arteries, clot formation, raise the LDL cholesterol, and lower the HDL cholesterol. There are no safe tobacco products.

Stress

Stress appears to contribute to heart disease in complex and as yet unclear ways. There appears to be "good" stress, such as the stress associated running a successful and fulfilling business. There appears to be "bad" stress associated with overwhelming challenges that lead to frustration and hopelessness. How much of a blend of these stresses occur in a any given situation is impossible to determine. Suffice to say, "bad" stress can contribute to elevated cholesterol, inflammation of arteries, and an increase in blood pressure, blood sugar, adrenaline, cortisol and clotting factors. All of these factors can promote coronary disease and heart attacks.

The Missing Links to Heart Disease

What other factors could explain the development of heart disease in people without the traditional risk factors? Why do almost half of the people getting heart disease not have the traditional risk factors? Remember the Dick Butkus story? He had few (if any) of the traditional risk factors, a story similar to half the people with heart disease.

Over the past decade, emerging risk factors have been identified. When these new risk factors are added to all people who develop heart disease, we then have an explanation for about 85% to 90% of those that develop coronary artery disease. Berkeley Heart Labs have been on the forefront in identifying these risk factors and developing readily available blood tests for these risk factors.

- HDL cholesterol that is ineffective (low subtype HDL_{2b})
- LDL cholesterol particles that are small and dense in size
- Lp (a)
- Homocysteine
- Inflammation: CRP and PLAC

The above risk factors are part of an Advanced Lipid Panel. The idea is to try to determine underlying causes for the coronary disease so that medications can be tailored to treat more specifically the cause.

Everyone with coronary disease, whether it is a very high coronary calcium score on EBCT scan, or someone who had a heart attack, stent, or surgery, will benefit from being on a cholesterol-lowering medications. The idea is to determine which one type of cholesterol medication would be best, or should there be a combination of medications to give the best chance at preventing the disease from progressing? If we break down the Advanced Lipid Panel results, we can fine-tune the medication selection.

The Advanced Lipid Panel breakdown

• HDL cholesterol subtypes

HDL is referred to as the good cholesterol because it acts as a scavenger, cleaning (in a sense) the inner lining of the arteries, removing the cholesterol-filled plaque, and bringing it back to the liver where it is removed. Most drug studies have focused mainly on the LDL cholesterol, the so-called bad cholesterol that brings cholesterol from the liver and deposits it in the lining of the arteries. The reason why LDL cholesterol has been more of a focus is due to the fact that it is easier to change the levels of LDL in your blood than it is to change the HDL levels. The trend now is coming around to paying more attention to HDL levels.

It turns out that HDL is not just one homogenous molecule. HDL is made up of numerous subunits. When the typical Lipid panel is ordered, a single number is given for the total HDL level. It can be that the HDL total is high, which you want (the higher the better), but you may have more plaque by EBCT calcium score than someone with a low normal HDL level. How can this be?

It seems that only one subunit of the HDL molecule, the HDL_{2b}, is the subunit that actually does the scavenging or cleaning of the artery. So, your total HDL may be high, but the HDL_{2b}, the portion that actually does the cleaning, may be low. So, on the surface it looks like you are protected by the high HDL level, when in fact the protective power of your HDL is weak.

It has often been thought (especially in women) that a high or very high HDL level protects them even if they have a high total cholesterol. Often, then, the high total cholesterol is not treated because it is thought that the high HDL is protecting that person. If a high calcium score on EBCT scan is noted, or the person had a coronary event, then measuring the HDL subtype is important.

If the HDL_{2b} subtype is < 20%, then *niacin* or a *fibrate* type of cholesterol medicine is needed to raise the HDL_{2b} unit to protect from further progression of heart disease. That is, you want to not only increase the total amount of HDL cholesterol, but you want to increase the *quality* of the HDL cholesterol by increasing the HDL_{2b} subunit which is actually the particle that scavenges or cleans the arteries.

- **LDL cholesterol size**

The LDL cholesterol is commonly referred to as the "bad cholesterol". The LDL carries cholesterol through the blood stream from the liver (where it is manufactured) to the inner lining (endothelium) of the arteries.

The higher the LDL level, the higher the risk of developing hardening of the coronary arteries, as well as other arteries of the body. It turns out that the *size* of the LDL particle is also important.

The smaller the overall size of the individual molecules, the more likely the LDL will cause plaque buildup. So why is it important to know the *size* of the LDL particle as well as the total *amount* of the LDL molecule? It is important to know size and amount because a *statin* type of cholesterol-lowering drug is very effective in changing the total amount of LDL, but niacin is the most effective in shifting the size of the LDL to larger LDL particle size, making the LDL less prone to cause plaque.

Niacin also reduces the LDL amount, but less effectively than statins. So, for the best treatment of plaque identified by EBCT scanning, you may need just a statin if the LDL quantity is high and the size is normal, or a statin and niacin if the amount of LDL is high and the size of the LDL is small. This is state of the art. (See figure below.)

• **Lipoprotein (a) called Lp(a)**

This is a little protein strand that attaches to the LDL molecule. When Lp(a) levels are high, the LDL molecule is more likely to enter the artery lining and cause plaque formation. Even if the total LDL is normal, if there is a lot of Lp(a) attached, the LDL becomes more potent in causing plaque. It turns out that high Lp(a) may be the only abnormality to explain the plaque formation in some people. The Lp(a) does not seem to be diet related; instead, it is genetically determined and found more frequently in certain ethnic backgrounds. More importantly, lowering Lp(a) is difficult but is best treated with niacin, less so with fibrates and hardly lowered at all with statins. However, if the total LDL is brought down, it does lower the potential risk for plaque even if the total amount of Lp(a) remains the same. So, for state-of-the-art treatment, a high Lp(a) needs to be determined and treated appropriately. (See figure follow)

• **Homocysteine**

This is a breakdown product of protein. Proteins are composed of amino acids. Amino acids can break down or metabolize into other amino acids. The breakdown requires the work of enzymes, some of which require certain B vitamins to function normally. Homocysteine builds up if certain enzymes are deficient or the required vitamins are deficient. An excess of Homocysteine has been associated with hardening of the arteries. The treatment for high Homocysteine is high doses of vitamin B_6 (pyridoxine), vitamin B_{12} (cyanocobalamine), and folic acid. Recent studies show that there is progression of coronary calcium seen on serial EBCT scanning if the homocysteine level is greater than 12. (See figure to follow)

• Inflammatory markers CRP, MPO and PLAC

These markers are not fat or cholesterol related. It is thought that the underlying process that starts plaque formation and plaque rupture leading to heart attacks is an underlying inflammation of the lining of the arteries. When inflammation is high, certain proteins are formed in the blood and the liver in response to this inflammation. The higher or more intense the inflammation, the higher the markers. The higher the inflammation, the more *likely* a heart attack. CRP (C-reactive protein) and the PLAC test (which detects an enzyme called lipoprotein-associated phospholipase A_2) measure this generalized inflammation. MPO is myelopeoxidase, another enzyme produced by white blood cells in response to inflammation of the arteries. It appears to be a more specific marker for arterial inflammation than CRP. Does it mean you are certain to have a heart attack if they are elevated? No! The usefulness is deciding what to do in people with borderline elevated cholesterol. If the CRP or PLAC is high and the cholesterol slightly elevated, then it would be prudent to treat the cholesterol, because it puts you at higher risk for a heart attack than the same level of cholesterol would if the CRP were normal. The treatment for high CRP and PLAC is aspirin and a statin.

• Bacterial Infection

There is some evidence that bacterial infections may play a role in causing coronary artery plaque. The most notable bacteria are Chlamydia pneumoniae (not the same as the Chlamydia that is sexually transmitted and causes genital infections), which cause pneumonia and upper respiratory infections. C. pneumoniae is transmitted by droplets during coughing. The bacteria have been isolated from plaque removed from coronary arteries. It is quite possible that the bacteria cause inflammation of the inner lining of the artery, leading to plaque formation. The relationship between heart attacks and Chlamydia has been inconsistent.

Studies treating heart-attack victims with antibiotics like azithromax have failed to show a reduction in subsequent heart attacks in those who took antibiotics, compared to those who did not take antibiotics. Perhaps the antibiotic dosages were not adequate, or the antibiotics need to be taken months or years before a heart attack. At present there is not enough evidence to recommend antibiotics if plaque is found on EBCT heart scans, nor is there evidence that testing for Chlamydia is useful. However, there probably is some relationship between some infections and coronary artery disease. Some time in the future this relationship will be better known.

Summary of Treatment for Cholesterol and Emerging Risk Factors

- Small LDL: niacin-fibrates-diet
- HDL_{2b} < 20%: niacin-fibrates
- Lp (a) > 20: niacin-fibrates- L-carnitine
- Homocysteine > 10: folic acid, vitamins B_6 and B_{12}
- HDL low: niacin-fibrates-exercise
- High Trig: niacin-fibrates-statins-fish oil
- High LDL: statins-niacin-resins
- High CRP, MPO and PLAC: statins-aspirin

Medications to Lower Cholesterol

DRUG CATEGORY	HOW THEY WORK SOME	COMMON AGENTS
Statins	Statins block the production of cholesterol.	Lovastatin, pravastatin, simvastatin, fluvastatin, atorvastatin, cerivastatin
Niacin	Niacin reduces the liver's ability to produce very low-density lipoprotein, the precursor of LDL.	Nicotinic acid, niacin extended-release (Niaspan), niacin (Slo-Niacin)
Fibrates	Fibrates activate an enzyme that speeds the breakdown of triglycerides in the blood.	Clofibrate (Atromid), gemfibrozil (Lopid), fenofibrate (Tricor)
Bile Acid Sequestrants	These drugs bind with bile acids (which are made from cholesterol) in the intestines and remove them in the stool. More cholesterol is then used by the liver to make bile acids.	Cholestyramine, colestipol
Cholesterol Absorption	They decrease total serum and LDL cholesterol levels by inhibiting absorption of cholesterol from the intestinal tract.	Ezetimibe (Zetia) is currently the only one approved from this category.

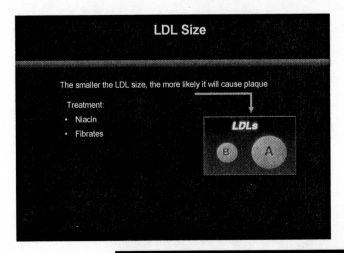

LDL Size

The smaller the LDL size, the more likely it will cause plaque

Treatment:
- Niacin
- Fibrates

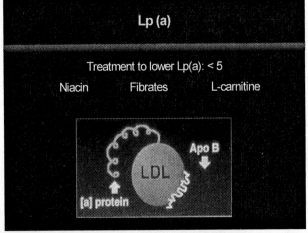

Lp (a)

Treatment to lower Lp(a): < 5

Niacin   Fibrates   L-carnitine

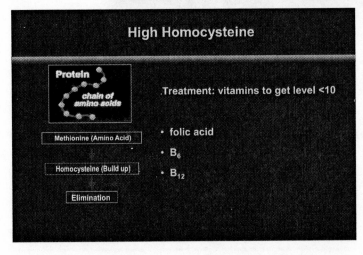

High Homocysteine

Treatment: vitamins to get level <10

- folic acid
- B_6
- B_{12}

10

Am I Doomed

by My Parents' Fate?

Most studies point to an increased risk for having heart disease if a parent or sibling developed symptoms of heart disease (that is, they had a heart attack, coronary bypass, PTCA or stent, or sudden cardiac death) before 55 years of age. Family history is important, but if you take the appropriate measures, you may not be doomed to the fate of your family. Somehow, genetics makes us susceptible to the known risks of heart disease.

The inner lining of the artery, called the endothelium, becomes sensitive to whatever is irritating it. The irritants may be the effects of cigarette smoke, the increase force of high blood pressure, or the increased irritation of high cholesterol circulating through the blood stream. The lining develops minor fissures and cracks in it that make for a focus for plaque formation.

However, you may not have inherited that sensitivity to these irritants, which may explain why only 40-50% of those with high cholesterol develop heart disease. On the other hand, you may have inherited a tendency to be very susceptible to these factors, which may explain why half of all heart attack victims have normal cholesterol; that is, a cholesterol level that is considered "normal" for the general population is at a level that will cause plague in a lining that is genetically susceptible to it. The level is too high for this particular person.

So how do we sort it out? One of the best uses for the EBCT screening exam is in patients with normal or near-normal cholesterol levels who also have a family history of heart disease. You can answer two questions: Did they inherit the tendency for heart disease? Should the *normal* cholesterol be treated with medications? If an EBCT scan shows significant calcium (either by total calcium score or percentile score), then they have inherited this tendency for early heart disease and the *normal* cholesterol should be treated with cholesterol medications.

This is a very important finding. By knowing that there is heart disease, the appropriate medications can be started and there is a very high probability that a cardiac event can be prevented. The plaque can be partially reversed, or stabilized, to prevent it from rupturing and causing a heart attack or progressing to an extent to where surgery or stents are needed.

If the EBCT scan shows no calcium in the coronary arteries, then there can be peace of mind. This person does not need to take cholesterol medications at this time, and the scan can be repeated in four to five years. That does not mean that a prudent diet, exercise, and modifying other risk factors like smoking or high blood pressure can be ignored. No coronary calcium does mean that there is a low probability of developing heart disease over the next five years if a prudent lifestyle is followed.

Can heart disease be prevented or reversed?

There is ample evidence to indicate that with proper diet, exercise, and medications to modify risk factors, heart disease can be prevented. Of course, it is not possible to prevent clinical disease in everyone, but it is possible to delay the onset of disease in most people. If you are otherwise destined to have a heart attack in your fifties, and it is delayed until your seventies, that is a more than worthwhile reason to modify your approach to heart disease as outlined in *The OC Heart Diet*.

There are numerous medical studies of various types conducted over the past fifteen years that show coronary artery disease can also be reversed. These are called angiographic studies. Patients had invasive coronary angiograms that revealed a narrowing of the coronary arteries. They were then placed on various cholesterol-lowering drugs (depending on the study). A number of years later the coronary angiogram was repeated and regression of the coronary narrowing was seen.

There have also been diet and lifestyle studies showing that reduced-fat diet, weight loss, and exercise prevent cardiac events and can reverse heart disease.

The OC Heart Diet program does it all!

The OC Heart Diet will benefit you if you have never had a heart problem, and it will benefit you even if you have had a cardiac event (a *cardiac event* means a heart attack or the need for a coronary stent or coronary bypass surgery). The way to look at it is that you had a cardiac event, you survived the event, and now the goal is to prevent another.

The diet and exercise concepts in *The OC Heart Diet* will work just as well for you. When you have a cardiac event, you unfortunately identified your heart disease at a more advanced stage than the person without symptoms who discovers their heart disease by having calcium on an EBCT heart scan. However, the underlying processes are the same in those who have had a cardiac event and those without a cardiac event but have coronary calcium on the EBCT heart scan. In one case the atherosclerosis was picked up sooner before stents or surgery was needed or a heart attack occurred.

In both circumstances, it is important to try to determine the cause of the disease and then to be on the proper medications, diet, and exercise to prevent the coronary disease from progressing. Unless something in the lifestyle changes, the disease will surely progress. It's not uncommon for a patient who had coronary bypass surgery at age 50 to reason that it will take forty or fifty more years before they need another surgery, since it took fifty years to get to the first one! If you have had a cardiac event or have very high calcium scores, you need the most vigorous risk modifications. Plaque can sometimes double in volume each year if risk factors are not vigorously treated. The fifty-year-old person who had bypass surgery will have his bypass grafts close in five to ten years if all the risk factors are not modified.

The future of heart testing

As mentioned earlier, imaging the heart presents unique challenges compared to tests to image other organs of the body. The speed of the *EBCT* heart scan makes it a very specialized CT scan for screening heart disease.

Whenever attempts are made to screen people for any type of disease, especially a disease like heart disease (which is so deadly and the most wide-spread of any known disease), the tools used to screen for the disease must meet these criteria:

- Extremely safe (meaning very low radiation)

- Relatively inexpensive (cost is less than most stress tests)

- Very accurate (coronary calcium means coronary disease)

- Large body of scientific evidence validating the benefits (thousands of scientific papers on EBCT scans)

- Large body of scientific evidence of how to modify the disease process if disease is found

EBCT scans are the only technology to meet these criteria when *screening* for coronary disease. *EBCT scans are the gold standard.* Basically, for now and long into the future, EBCT scans will be the preferred scan for coronary calcium screening because of speed, low radiation doses, and the vast number of studies performed using EBCT scans.

However, technology is rapidly changing and newer varieties of CT scans will undoubtedly be developed that will compete with the EBCT scan for heart imaging. However, a modified EBCT scanner, referred to, for lack of a better name, as *super EBCT* is possibly in the near future, having the advantage of low radiation, and superior detail and may be the preferred tool for CT angiograms as well as for screening.

Most people have now heard about the *64-slice CT*. These newer conventional CT scans are called *multi-slice* CT scanners. A "slice" essentially refers to how many tiny lenses are in the CT camera. The more lenses or slices, the greater the picture detail and the more surface area of the heart covered in a certain period of time. The more slices or lenses, the higher the radiation dose.

There is a great deal of confusion with the public since recent public demonstrations of the 64-slice CT on national TV shows like *The Oprah Winfrey Show* and *The Today Show*. These shows demonstrated *CT angiograms,* which required intravenous dye injection and large doses of radiation. CT angiograms are *not screening tests* and should only be performed except on the advice of a physician and for particular reasons. This distinction is not made clear on any of the shows which demonstrated this technology. Due this confusion, people are now calling for 64-slice CT scans for screening on themselves, or CT angiograms for screening.

The bottom line is this: 64-slice CT scans are not acceptable for screening due to the extremely high radiation dose, and less than optimal calcium visualization. Other multi-slice CT scanners, commonly referred to as 16-slice CT scans have similar characteristics and are also not suitable for coronary screening.

The multi-slice CT will, therefore, be less desirable for screening the general population for coronary calcium because of the higher radiation doses. Also, there are few studies correlating the amount of calcium detected with the multi-slice scanner and what this calcium score means as far as the patient's chance of having a heart attack or other cardiac event.

The 64-slice CT, however, is an excellent scanner for CT angiograms. A CT angiogram is when a dye is injected into a vein during the time the CT or EBCT scan is performed. A detailed picture of the coronary arteries and coronary bypass grafts is seen. These are called *angiograms*. Presently, only EBCT coronary angiograms are approve for CT coronary angiography, but the 64-slice will shortly receive approval. However, although neither has the detailed image of invasive coronary angiograms, the CT angiogram is non-invasive, quick and relatively safer than invasive angiograms.

In summary, an EBCT scan is the screening tool of choice for coronary calcium and full-body screening. If your doctor requests that you have a CT angiogram, request it on an EBCT scan or 64-slice CT. Also request that it be done at a center under the direction of cardiologists with experience in CT angiography. Having performed many hundreds of CT angiograms, I can attest that at times they can be very challenging to interpret.

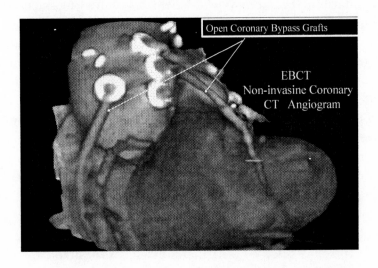

CT Angiogram Using an EBCT Scanner
Courtesy of OC Vital Imaging

Putting it all together

Start with the EBCT scan to see if you have heart disease. This will be the start of your roadmap. Look in Appendix A for current EBCT scanning centers near you. If available in your area, make sure that the scan center uses an EBCT scan and not a conventional multislice CT scan. They are not the same! Medication recommendations and other testing are based on the amount (if any) of coronary calcium.

• Know your coronary calcium score and percentile.

• Diet plan

Next, read and incorporate the changes described in the diet section of this book. This diet program will benefit everyone, of all ages, with or without heart disease. The results are remarkable. You will look better, feel better, and have an eating program that is easy to maintain for life.

• Exercise plan

Next, read the section on exercise. Choose an exercise plan that fits your needs. The exercise programs are flexible in the sense they can be modified for any lifestyle, from the couch potato to the elite athlete. Remember, if you have been sedentary or have coronary calcium, check with your doctor first. You may need an exercise stress test before undertaking a vigorous exercise program.

• Choosing a doctor can save your life

It is important to work with a doctor who understands the value of the EBCT heart scan results. The recommendations and report that should be provided with your scan will easily guide you and your doctor in subsequent testing and cholesterol goals. See chapter 8 for a sample report. If your doctor feels that coronary calcium in *your arteries* is not important to your future, you need to find a physician who does. Your life may depend on it.

Part II

Food in the proper balance can have a dramatic, positive effect on all of the body's systems, but most dramatically on the heart. *The OC Heart Diet* weight-loss program is a balanced diet consisting of 50% low-glycemic carbohydrates, 25% proteins, and 25% essential fats. This is the most natural diet available today.

The OC Heart Diet focus is on low-glycemic carbohydrates. The physiology of low-glycemic nutrition is powerful, yet simple. Foods that have a low-glycemic index are best because they promote a slow to moderate rise in blood sugar and insulin after a meal—factors that help keep hunger in check. These same factors also encourage the body to dissolve body fat by converting it into energy, while facilitating stress management and immune functions. Low-glycemic foods are also premium fuel for athletes and active people. According to a recent study at San Jose State University, low-glycemic carbohydrates can increase endurance and stamina by as much as 60%.

The OC Heart Diet is a guide to better nutrition through your evolving caloric requirements as the composition and metabolic rate of your body allow you to achieve a safe and effective weight-management program. With proper understanding, an implementation *The OC Heart Diet* will provide you with a proven way to achieve maximum fat burning and cardiovascular efficiency. This new diet of nutrition and exercise maximizes results and minimizes the confusion prevalent among so many diets being promoted today.

11

The Secret is 50/25/25

T*he OC Heart Diet* program is an effective and practical weight-loss program intervention. The following is a de scription of the 50/25/25 low-glycemic nutrition program, as set forth in the OC Heart Diet Program, along with the scientif-ic support behind it. The nutritional aspects of *The OC Heart Diet* are to achieve a balance of 50% low-glycemic carbohydrates, 25% protein, and 25% essential fats at each meal. It is the most direct path to wise eating.

The importance of 50/25/25 ratios are explained in the follow-ing chapter.These figures are important to understanding the nu-tritional goals of *The OC Heart Diet.* It helps you achieve the necessary lifestyle changes to bring about and maintain a healthy level of weight loss while maximizing energy levels and lean body mass.

The OC Heart Diet is a personalized weight-loss program tai-lored specifically for each individual. The program designs a schedule as to the proper daily caloric intake of the correct amounts of high-quality proteins, low-glycemic carbohydrates, and essential fats. This adaptability becomes a powerful tool to remedy the pervasive problem of obesity.

Fighting "the battle of the bulge" is a huge industry. With so much information on fats in the news, it's not surprising many Americans get confused. This confusion came to a head in 2000 when studies and surveys continued to show that Americans are heavier than ever before, even though they are reducing the percentage of calories consumed from fat. How can this be?

Popular diet books and the media immediately targeted carbohydrates as the bad guys and labeled them "fattening". This is completely in opposition to the major health groups such as the *American Medical Association, American Heart Association, American Cancer Society*, and *the National Institute of Health's* whole philosophy of "healthy eating". This is a pretty impressive group of experts. In addition, what was ignored is the fact that in 1994 the average American consumed 40,000 calories per year— or 126 calories more per day than they did in 1990.

This has increased even more today. The correct message should be that excess calories from any source—protein, fats, and carbohydrates—result in increased body fat.

In *The OC Heart Diet* program, we found that taking in fewer calories than one burns, finding foods that have a low-glycemic index, and consuming the correct amounts of macronutrients at the proper times is best because it promotes a slow-to-moderate rise in blood sugar and insulin after each meal, allows for maximum fat loss and increased energy levels, and keeps hunger and cravings in check. Macronutrients are carbohydrates, proteins, and fats. Micronutrients are vitamins and minerals.

Research at Boston Children's Hospital has shown that a low-glycemic diet can reduce hunger by as much as 83%. These same factors also encourage the body to dissolve body fat by converting it into energy. A team at San Jose State University has proven that low-glycemic carbohydrates eaten before endurance training can increase exercise time to exhaustion by 60%, while dramatically increasing fat oxidation.

Low-glycemic foods are also an integral part of improved cardiovascular health. *The Harvard Nurses Study* firmly established that a low-glycemic diet could reduce heart attacks by 50%. This type of low-glycemic nutrition has broad support within the medical community.

Simply put, an individually designed nutrition program, whose core principle is low-glycemic nutrition, reflects the overwhelming weight of scientific evidence relating to the long-term effects of protein to low-glycemic carbohydrate to essential fat ratios in solving the problem of obesity in this nation (both adults and children), the onset of Type II Diabetes, and optimizing the performance of active individuals—from the "weekend warrior" to the professional and world-class athlete.

Why The OC Heart Diet program works

Integrative medicine views the human being as composed of mind, body, and spirit. All three of these components depend upon a specific and scheduled input of nutrients in order to survive at an optimal level. The body and mind become healthy physically and emotionally when regular exercise, balanced eating, and proper supplementation are made a daily part of the individual's lifestyle.

The OC Heart Diet program is designed for the man or woman who has decided to take charge of his or her health by becoming fit. Good health is not the result of better health care. It is the result of a better lifestyle. This system provides the practitioner with the necessary tools to give the individual the ability to make the lifesaving changes that will have a significant impact on his or her health.

Over 90% of the American public does not participate in a disciplined program of regular exercise, balanced nutrition, and proper supplementation. The OC Diet Program allows individuals to become a part of the growing percentage of Americans who are taking charge of their own health by joining in a resolution to "do something about my condition."

You can arm yourself with a complete arsenal of what is necessary to maintain a healthy person, a higher quality of life, and the energy to accomplish anything that you want.

The OC Heart Diet is a safe and effective alternative to many of the marginal diet plans offered today. The unfounded assumptions supporting high-glycemic-carbohydrate/low-fat diets, low-carb/high-protein/low-fat programs, and the high-protein/ high-fat regimens have actually limited goal realizations while having negative health effects as well. Individuals can utilize macronutrients (proteins, fats, and carbohydrates) to orchestrate peak-energy/performance levels and maximize fat loss.

A precise balance of 50% low-glycemic carbohydrates, 25% protein, and 25% essential fats at each meal supports the healthy function of the body's systems and creates a safe platform for caloric reduction and the reduction of excess body fat. All of this is individualized to age, weight, height, body-fat percentage, lean-muscle mass, and activity levels.

A simple goal

The goal of *The OC Heart Diet* is simple: it is to create a safe and effective weight-management program that allows you to achieve maximum health and wellness.

The OC Heart Diet's goal is to provide the individual with the means to individually calculate the food, meal replacements, and supplements in the proper balance, according to your unique profile. Independent university and clinical studies have shown that this balance, if done in a personalized manner, can have a dramatic positive effect on all systems of the body.

Most individuals are out of balance in their eating and supplementation habits, and this can have a negative effect on their vital systems, whether they are sedentary or active. This system of a 50/25/25 low-glycemic nutrition plan represents a breakthrough in nutrition based on research at such prestigious institutions as Harvard University, Stanford, San Jose State, and other institutions.

With eight of ten risk factors directly related to diet, a properly balanced weight-loss program has been shown to significantly reduce the prevalence of obesity, heart disease, hypertension, cancer, elevated cholesterol, diabetes, hypoglycemia, and alcohol abuse. Furthermore, proper nutrition plays a major role in reducing illness and increasing productivity, concentration, and focus.

In the athlete, it has been shown to increase lean muscle, eliminate fat, increase endurance by as much as 60%, and significantly reduce recovery time.

What The OC Heart Diet program can accomplish

The human body is a miraculous creation. If properly fueled, it naturally manages its own mass, which allows maximum performance and protects it from the ravages of degenerative disease.

Our program allows a better balance of nutrients at each meal. This enables the user to maximize the body's ability to burn stored body fat as energy without sacrificing lean-muscle mass, while improving overall health and decreasing the risk of degenerative diseases.

The program provides a macronutrient balance, which, we repeat, includes 50% low-glycemic carbohydrates, 25% proteins, and 25% essential fats. Today, the typical American diet contains 12% protein, 51% high-glycemic carbohydrates, and 37% fats. The realized benefits of eating in 50/25/25 manner are:

- Increased fat loss
- Increased lean muscle
- Increased energy levels
- Stabilized blood sugar
- Increased endurance levels
- Reduced stress

How The OC Heart Diet program increases fat loss

The OC Heart Diet program increases fat loss by creating an environment in which the participant is ingesting the correct amount of calories, the correct ratio of macronutrients, at the correct times of the day. The typical American diet is too high in not only calories but also saturated fats and simple sugars. The latter are often referred to as high-glycemic-index carbohydrates.

It is a fact that excess amounts of calories are always stored as fat. This process, combined with the intake of high-glycemic-index carbohydrates, increases blood sugar levels significantly, which in turn increases circulating levels of the hormone insulin. In turn, this leads to a drop in blood-glucose levels that causes frequent hunger pangs, cravings, and a loss of energy.

The result of ingesting excessive amounts of calories, fluctuating insulin levels, and excessive intake of dietary fat is the activation of the body's fat-storage mechanism. When you take in too many calories, you simply trigger the storage bin.

In fact, over consumption, increased insulin, and high amounts of dietary fat are three of the most potent stimulators of this extremely important mechanism. The more active this mechanism, the more fat enters the fat cells and stays there. This is why in order to reduce body fat, you must reduce the activity of this mechanism.

The OC Heart Diet does just that. By personalizing caloric intake, reducing dietary fat from 37% to 25% (the amount currently being recommended), reducing dietary, high-glycemic carbohydrates (those that produce excessive amounts of insulin) and replacing them with 50% low-glycemic carbohydrates, and consuming 25% high-quality proteins, you come out with a personalized caloric intake.

The OC Heart Diet decreases the body's fat-storage activity, thereby allowing less fat to go into fat cells, while at the same time allowing more fat to leave the fat cell and be utilized for energy throughout the day, as well as during physical activity. The overall results will astound you.

The only mechanism that allows for continual fat loss while simultaneously maintaining lean-muscle mass is a weight-loss plan that is completely individualized—one which provides the exact ratios of proteins, fats, and carbohydrates, the correct number of calories to be consumed, and at what times and in what amounts meals should be eaten. You end up forcing accountability through weekly reassessments.

In summary, *The OC Heart Diet* program increases body fat loss by creating the proper physiological and psychological environment on an individual basis, optimizing the body's utilization of fat, and maintaining lean-muscle mass. Sounds too easy, right? It is THE solution, and properly followed the result is weight loss.

12

Comparison to Other Approaches

The *OC Heart Diet* results in a simple-to-use program that addresses the basic biochemical causes of weight gain, weight management, maximum energy levels, increased performance, and decreased recovery from exertion. All of this is accomplished by controlling caloric intake and macronutrient ratios on an individual basis. In other words, it is based upon the most recent advances in human nutrition, performance, and biochemistry.

This plan applies to all individuals in every walk of life: from the obese to the professional and world-class athlete. On this program, in a matter of a few days those who follow it see dramatic improvements in their life. To fully understand the uniqueness of the impact that this approach has, we need to first examine other existing diet programs. Let's compare them.

The most aggressive weight-loss programs—and potentially the most dangerous—are the liquid-protein diet programs. These programs, which work on the principle of ketosis (these are, therefore, called ketogenic diets), are either physician supervised or purchased over the counter in drug and health-food stores. Ketosis means the build-up of ketonic bodies that form when fats are not completely metabolized when carbohydrates are inadequate.

In theory, if the body is supplied with adequate protein but very low amounts of carbohydrates and virtually no fat (or a lot of fat, as in Dr. Atkins' Diet), then you see rapid weight loss. We emphasize the term "weight loss" because most of this initial loss is due to water loss, not fat loss. As much as a startling 50% of the weight lost is metabolically active lean-body mass. Part of it is muscle.

Furthermore, ketogenic diets deplete glycogen stores in the liver. Glycogen is sugar stored in the liver and muscle that is used for energy. Without liver glycogen, it is impossible to maintain adequate blood sugar levels. We repeat once again: the brain requires massive levels of blood sugar (i.e., glucose) to sustain itself.

If glucose is not released from the liver due to glycogen depletion, the body will begin to convert the protein from the liquid weight-loss formula into glucose for the brain's continual glucose demands. Remember, the brain is a hog when it comes to glucose.

Within two to three hours after drinking a liquid-protein drink, most of the protein has been converted to blood glucose in a process known as gluconeogenesis.

However, the brain still requires additional glucose for normal functioning. Where does it go foraging for this? It forces your body to convert muscle tissue in its demand for blood sugar, causing loss of muscle and organ tissue. Why are muscle and organ mass cannibalized to make additional glucose instead of fat? This is due to the ketosis inhibiting the release of glucagons, which are required to release stored body fat.

This is why long-term weight loss on ketogenic diets is one to two pounds per week, but of that amount as much as 50% of the weight loss may be muscle and organ tissue. These problems make it necessary for any ketogenic diet (i.e., quick weight-loss program) to be followed only under a physician's supervision.

The OC Heart Diet Program eliminates this need, making it an ideal program for a broad spectrum of participants from weight loss to world-class athletes or just plain svelte bodies.

Optimal calorie intake and the aging process

Determining the optimal caloric needs for a person will have a dramatic effect on the aging process. For decades it has been known that caloric restriction (assuming all nutrient levels are maintained) results in a greatly increased lifespan for every animal species studied, as well as for humans. Not only is the lifespan increased, but the vitality of the animal is remarkably constant throughout its entire lifetime.

This should not be too surprising when you think of the stress caloric intake places on the body. Many people wrongly assume that the body will only absorb the calories it needs, and the rest will pass merrily out of the system. Not so. Unfortunately, the opposite is true. The human body is a remarkable piece of engineering that absorbs virtually every calorie placed in the mouth.

Once these calories are absorbed, the body has to do something with them. The body's ability to store carbohydrates as glycogen and store protein as muscle mass is greatly limited. However, the body has an unfortunate and unlimited capacity for turning excess protein and carbohydrates into fat, and storing it as excess body fat with the greatest of ease.

Furthermore, the individual cells have to work fairly hard to make these biochemical transformations of excess protein and carbohydrates into fat. The more calories that are being shoved into the body, the faster the basic machinery has to work to convert these calories into something that the body can use or store. This is analogous to an Indy 500 racing car. Traveling at 20 miles per hour, this marvel of mechanical engineering can last for decades. Increase the speed to 200 miles per hour, and the car is unlikely to remain functional for two hours.

The cells of the human body are no different. They appear to have a built-in biological clock with a self-termination mechanism. The faster the clock turns, the more rapidly the termination time is reached. As an example, human skin cells divide fifty times, and then simply stop making any further divisions and scale off the body.

You can make these same cells divide thirty times, then freeze them for years. When the cells are thawed out, they divide another twenty times and then stop. Once you reach the built-in biological clock limit, the game stops.

Obviously, the faster cells metabolize excess caloric intake, the more the clock speeds up, because the micro factories of the cell (i.e., the enzymes) wear out, requiring increased cell divisions to replace them. Conversely, slowing the clock down by supplying the optimal amount of calories moves the clock forward more slowly, extending one's lifespan.

Nutrients needed

These statements are only true if the body's nutrient needs are maintained. Nutrients include the vitamins and minerals that the body cannot synthesize. These are the micronutrients that you cannot obtain from food alone any longer. In some way they must be supplied by a balanced, individualized diet and proper supplementation.

Nutrients include essential amino acids—protein from eggs, seafood, fowl, meats, cottage cheese, or supplemental items —in addition from essential fatty acids and micronutrients. Notice that carbohydrates are not considered essential, because the body can synthesize carbohydrates from other sources.

Another aspect to be considered is the important criterion for slowing the aging process (which is not yet fully understood). This is hormonal balance. We believe that this is affected by macronutrient ratios and that it requires a precise, yet easily ascertained balance of protein to low-glycemic-carbohydrate to fat ratio.

If one compares the ratio of calories obtained from protein, low-glycemic carbohydrates, and essential fats required to achieve this favorable hormonal balance, it appears to be very different from the caloric intake recommended in other programs such as Pritikin, Atkins, and even the Government Food Pyramid.

13

Energy Levels–
Physical and Emotional

There are many factors that determine a person's energy levels on a daily basis; included in this are things both phys ical and emotional. Two of the strongest determinants include blood sugar (or blood glucose) levels and neurotransmitter levels in the brain.

This is what we are talking about. Low blood sugar levels (known also as hypoglycemia) produce fatigue by a process that is actually quite simple. Since the brain normally uses glucose as its sole source of energy, a low blood glucose level forces the brain to take action since it perceives such levels as a threat to proper functioning and, in a manner of speaking, it says to the body, "Relax, don't do anything that would require physical activity, because I need that glucose, not you." When the brain says this, it is shouted out. It is as if an alarm has gone off in your head, and it sends out the message with an accompanying shaking-fatigue sensation that causes you to search desperately for fuel. Your brain suddenly demands glucose, while you body is suffering from hunger.

Although this is an important survival mechanism for the human body overall, the results are still the same: fatigue or low energy levels. Practically speaking, diets high in calories from "high-glycemic" carbohydrates tend to propagate fluctuations in blood glucose levels and, subsequently, energy levels as well. This is a very real experience that all dieters know.

Those that are high protein/low carbohydrate have the same adverse effect on blood glucose/energy levels. Conversely, *The OC Heart Diet* program is a safe and effective alternative to many of the marginal diet plans offered today. The unfounded assumptions supporting high-glycemic-carbohydrate/low-fat diets, low-carb/high-protein/low-fat programs, and the high-protein/high-fat regimens have actually limited goal realizations while having negative health effects as well. Individuals can utilize macronutrients (proteins, fats, and carbohydrates) to orchestrate peak energy and performance levels and maximize fat loss.

When the brain demands fuel for energy, it has to be met, or there is a near rebellion. This is why you have to balance the intake with a precise balance of 50% low-glycemic carbohydrates, 25% protein, and 25% essential fats at each meal to satisfy this demand. If you follow carefully the proper fuel intake, then there is a healthy function of the body's systems that creates a safe platform for caloric reduction and the reduction of excess body fat.

When you do this properly, all of this will be individualized to age, weight, height, body-fat percentage, lean-muscle mass, and activity levels. Without a custom-tailored intake of food, the diet won't work.

Our diet program helps control blood sugar levels within a more narrow range than with other fuel-intake programs. It allows for energy levels to be maintained throughout the day. In short, the brain is not desperate for glucose when you follow your specifically designed program of 50/25/25. If you remain on this custom-designed program, you will experience significant weight loss while maximizing overall health and wellness.

This plan also helps regulate neurotransmitter levels, amino-acid-based activators that influence energy levels significantly. For example, research has shown that people experience fatigue after a meal high in "high-glycemic" carbohydrates because such a meal increases a particular neurotransmitter known as serotonin, which (amongst its many functions) induces sleep. The body wants to rest as a result of high-glycemic carbohydrate intake. You have experienced this and perhaps had no idea why you suddenly wanted to take a nap.

Carbohydrates do this by increasing insulin levels, which in turn alter amino-acid levels in the bloodstream. This alteration causes more tryptophan to enter the brain, allowing the brain to manufacture more serotonin, resulting in increased tiredness.

Our program is designed to keep serotonin levels in check and provide the right amount of high-quality protein with the right amino acids, thereby preventing interruptions in energy levels from the brain.

Increased endurance

When you follow this program, your body is eating macronutrients at correct, individualized ratios, at the proper times and in the correct number of calories. You will also retain blood glucose levels and maintain glycogen stores in the muscles and liver; thereby setting up the mechanism for utilizing more fat for energy, both at rest and during exercise. In this way endurance can be greatly enhanced by sparing muscle glycogen, which serves as the body's high-octane fuel.

For example, if muscle glycogen levels become depleted, a person's endurance or performance is greatly reduced and one falls short of what is expected. When the right amounts of proteins, low-glycemic carbohydrates, and essential fats are ingested in the proper amounts and at the correct times during the day, fat utilization is increased and muscle glycogen (your very special high-octane fuel) is spared, allowing your body to have increased endurance and performance.

Development of *The OC Heart Diet* program

Researchers at a variety of prestigious universities have focused their research efforts on how best to maximize fat loss, energy levels, endurance, recovery, and immune function, along with some other less essential aspects of the diet. This focus has given researchers an understanding of how caloric intake and the macronutrient composition of foods control the fat storage and burning mechanisms. This vital research thoroughly studied the effects in the above-named areas of the major nutrition plans in the marketplace today in order to ferret out the best of the best.

Those researchers had to delve into some rather unique areas in order to come up with a satisfactory answer to a problem that is becoming epidemic in this country, that of obesity. Among the items they included were drug-delivery principles, food technology, and endocrinology. The end result was the development of the 50/25/25 low-glycemic approach to weight loss.

Although it is exceptionally simple to use, the 50/25/25 low-glycemic approach is one of the major accomplishments of research into the areas of biotechnology where, for the first time, we found that precise dietary control of the macronutrients, supplements, and activity levels of an individual provided for a complete change in a number of physiological and psychological areas, thus allowing for better adherence to fuel intake.

This breakthrough program provides the opportunity for you to take control of how food affects your body. Instead of being controlled by food, whatever your goal—whether it be weight loss, more energy, better athletic performance, faster recovery, stronger immune system, or the many medical benefits gained by controlling the onset of insulin resistance and eliminating obesity—this 50/25/25 low-glycemic approach and the principles behind its development have become the foundation of our dietary strategy—a strategy that works!

Medical benefits

The benefits of controlling the onset of insulin resistance go to the very foundation of cardiovascular treatment and prevention. It is often assumed that insulin only affects blood sugar levels. Not so.

Unfortunately, an overproduction of insulin may lead to insulin resistance, a condition that may have a dramatic negative impact on cardiovascular health. This can happen primarily in the areas of cholesterol levels, hypertension, and the onset of diabetes. In each of these disease states, increased insulin levels create a feedback situation, making cells less responsive to insulin, thus creating the condition known as insulin resistance.

Type II diabetes (which accounts for over 90% of all types of diabetics and is now being seen in adolescents in epidemic numbers) is defined as an insulin-resistance disease. Any therapy that reduces insulin response will decrease the chances of insulin resistance, resulting in a normalization of blood sugar levels. *The OC Heart Diet's* ability to lower significantly the chances of insulin resistance and its occurrence has a significant, positive impact on Type II diabetics.

We need to also note that dietary cholesterol has relatively little effect on serum-cholesterol levels. This is because greater than 75% of the body's cholesterol comes from synthesis in the liver as opposed to diet.

There are two key enzymes that control the liver's synthesis of cholesterol. These are the twins, acetyl CoA carboxylase, and 3hydroxy-3-methylglutaryl-CoA (HMG CoA) reductase. The 50/25/25 approach to food consumption inhibits the activity of the enzyme acetyl CoA carboxylase that provides the necessary building block for cholesterol synthesis manufactured by the liver.

This is why a nutrition program that is properly balanced has a favorable impact in the area of promoting an overall decrease in the liver's synthesis of cholesterol. The end result may be a favorable reduction in serum cholesterol, especially for those individuals with chronically high serum-cholesterol levels.

There is some anecdotal research that indicates that insulin may have a stimulatory effect on another hormone known as aldosterone. It affects blood pressure. If aldosterone is activated, it can cause a preferential retention of sodium from the urine, which in turn promotes increased fluid retention necessary to dilute bound sodium (salt).

This is why, after eating a high-calorie, high-glycemic, carbohydrate meal, you notices significant water retention and weight gain, which is a distressing turn of events. The increased high-glycemic carbohydrate intake may cause increased insulin secretion. As a result, aldosterone is activated, promoting sodium retention, which, in turn, leads to increased water retention, which ultimately shows up as weight gain.

This is why hypertension, hyperlipidemia, Type II diabetes, and obesity are all associated with increased insulin response and insulin resistance. You want to know why people suffering from morbid obesity, who lose 100 pounds, no longer take medication for diabetes? By losing excess body fat (which can only be achieved by controlling caloric intake and the ratios of macronutrients), insulin resistance and the increased insulin levels are reduced, leading to a reduction, if not total elimination, of this disease.

It's not surprising that the primary physician's advice to the individual with high cholesterol, hypertension, or Type II diabetes is to lose weight. Unfortunately, most physicians can't explain why weight loss has such a beneficial effect, because they are not familiar with the critical role that the macronutrient ratio plays in cardiovascular conditions.

Controlling caloric intake and one's individual macronutrient ratio by using the 50/25/25 low-glycemic approach as delineated in this program may have major dietary impact on those risk parameters associated with heart disease.

Controlled insulin levels

To fully appreciate why the 50/25/25 low-glycemic approach represents such a revolutionary means for controlling the onset of insulin resistance, you must first examine the evolution of dieting and weight loss with humans.

Fasting was undoubtedly the first diet program known to man. Obviously, if you don't eat, weight loss will surely follow. Unfortunately, death is also a likely consequence of prolonged fasting.

The amazing thing about fasting is that after three to four days of no intake of fuel, the dieter experiences feelings of euphoria and a heightened sense of well being, even though the body is literally digesting itself by consuming with great frenzy its own muscle, organs, and brain in a sort of cannibalistic ritual. It becomes desperate to provide the building blocks necessary to make new protein, and supply glucose for the brain. Remember, the brain is the control center. It is the last fortress of defense against starvation.

In fact, this sense of well being is caused by ketone bodies during extreme fasting. If it continues, the body dies from heart failure caused by the body's own generation of these abnormal chemicals known as ketone bodies. Ketone bodies are the end products of the incomplete metabolism of fats in the absence of adequate amounts of carbohydrates. Ketone bodies can interact with the hypothalamus in the brain, not only to override hunger signals but also cause a slight state of euphoria.

The famous Indian leader, Gandhi, of the last century seemed to understand this phenomenon of a protein-sparing fast and could go for days without fuel. Of course, several times he nearly died, and most of the time he was extremely frail and fatigued.

The development of so-called "protein-sparing fasts" repre-sented the next logical step in the promotion of weight loss. Re-searchers hypothesized that if enough protein was supplied by the diet, the body would not degrade itself.

Furthermore, if adequate supplies of vitamins and minerals were also included, the benefits of fasting (i.e., rapid weight loss) could be maintained without the negative consequences (i.e., death). These diets still generated ketone bodies to overcome natu-ral hunger and were referred to as ketogenic diets.

Although the protein supplied was adequate to slow the abso-lute maximum loss of muscle mass, invariably large amounts of muscle loss (25% to 50%) in the total weight loss were reported with these programs. Given the potential for ketogenic diets to cause significant metabolic disturbances, they should only be tried under strict medical supervision.

Fat magnets

There are a host of these ketogenic diets on the market today. You know them by such brand names as Opti-Fast™ Medi-Fast™ Ultra Slim-Fast™ the Atkins Diet™ and any diet plan that is based on high-protein, low-carbohydrate eating. They work. You do lose weight!

Although these ketogenic diets work by causing rapid weight loss, nevertheless, invariably 90 to 95% of all users, once they resume consumption of regular food, regain all their weight and more. The reason this happens is that the fat cells adapt to the abnormal presence of ketone bodies and in essence become "fat magnets". Ketogenic weight-loss programs alter the enzymes in the fat cells, so the slightest increase in dietary fat is quickly shuttled to the fat cells.

Therefore, it is not surprising that any new eating habits created through behavior modification are useless in the face of these biochemical changes caused by ketogenic diets.

Carbohydrate packing

At the other end of the spectrum are those diets that supply more than adequate amounts of carbohydrates but are very low in calories due to reduced protein and fat intake. Examples of these diets are commonly found in most women's magazines. They consist of low-calorie, high-glycemic carbohydrate diets that tend to be characterized by the constant hunger and fatigue they create. These diets are based on the principle that weight loss and weight gain are simply a matter of calorie counting—very shortsighted for anyone wishing to maintain a steady weight loss.

This sort of diet works short term in a simplistic way. But, since the body is a very complex organism and every individual is unique, research has shown that macronutrient ratios are also important. The constant state of hunger and fatigue caused by these diets has been considered the price one pays for weight loss.

By consuming large amounts of complex carbohydrates containing fiber, it was hoped that the stomach would remain relatively full, thus retarding constant hunger. This creates constant cravings because of the imbalance of nutrients that the body is used to receiving. It's a fairly self-defeating program because of lack of adherence for any length of time.

Probably the best example of this type of diet is the *Pritikin*

Diet™. This program calls for 80% carbohydrates, 10% protein, and 10% fat. A well-known registered dietician wrote a best seller on the negative side effects suffered by those on this type of diet.

These high complex-carbohydrate diets also have a very low success rate, although long-term weight loss will occur if you can maintain the strict regimen required by these low-calorie, high-carbohydrate diets. Another complicating factor is their exceptionally low fat intake, which contributes to potential long-term deficiencies in essential fatty acids.

The illogical extension of the complex-carbohydrate-diet principle is to simply put massive amounts of fiber into the stomach and let it expand. This is the basis for diets using capsules containing fibers (such as guar gum), which dramatically expand upon contact with water. Obviously, just from observation, you can see the potential difficulties that occur within the mechanisms of the body as a result of being on such a diet.

The set-point theory

You can alter genetically your predetermined set point, which is very easily done by utilizing a personalized weight-loss program that not only provides a proper eating plan but one that depends on weekly readjustments. It is a well-known fact that a good weight-loss program will cause small changes in an individual's profile every week.

In order to accelerate you through any set points, we have designed our system to hold you accountable monthly to new "daily caloric measurements". You then make adjustments to your program. Too many diets make the individual stay on a constant, unchanging program. In the long run it fails for most.

This leads to a slowing down of the results achieved by you and will ultimately result in a complete cessation somewhere down the line. This leads to overwhelming discouragement and the lack of adherence to the rapid-loss diet. The OC Heart Diet has reached an understanding of how to deal with one of the most powerful mechanisms that the body has for creating hunger and cravings. We'll let you in on this mystery.

The glucose hog

Too many carbohydrates, proteins, or fats will ultimately flood the body with excess calories and cause a spike in blood glucose levels. As glucose enters the bloodstream, your body releases insulin. Any excess glucose that your body cannot store as glycogen in the liver and muscles will be converted to fat. Moreover, insulin will also decrease blood sugar levels by removing glucose from the bloodstream. This is an important key to understanding the biochemical basis of hunger.

Secondly, the brain demands massive amounts of blood sugar for normal functioning. In fact, the brain is a "glucose hog", requiring nearly sixty times more glucose per pound of tissue than muscle.

This is why any drop in blood sugar levels will have a dramatic impact on brain function and efficiency. The brain will correct these dramatic drops in blood sugar by sending out signals for your body to consume fuel—sometimes in the form of a candy bar. This is the source of the typical carbohydrate cravings, or hunger, a person experiences two to three hours after an improperly balanced meal.

At the other end of the spectrum of the hunger-and-craving mechanism are those diets rich in protein but poor in carbohydrates. These diets are characterized by the insufficient intake of low-glycemic carbohydrates necessary to maintain blood sugar levels. However, the lack of carbohydrates leads to the generation of ketone bodies, which mask hunger.

The initial ketone-body formation causes the dull-to-severe headaches associated with ketogenic diets. Although hunger is masked, the brain continues to demand glucose. To satisfy the brain's craving for carbohydrates during ketosis, the body begins to convert protein from the meal (or diet shake) into blood sugar. This is a very expensive way to maintain blood sugar levels for the brain. This process continues for about two to three hours, after which most of the protein intake has been converted to blood sugar.

Unfortunately, the demands of the brain are still not fully satisfied, and now the body's muscle mass is broken down and converted into glucose to maintain adequate supplies of glucose for the brain.

As blood sugar levels drop, mental fatigue and light-headedness may set in. While weight loss is observed, much of it is at the expense of muscle mass—up to 50%. These are some of the reasons ketogenic diets require a physician's supervision and are not long-term, lifestyle changing.

Target zone

These various dilemmas, inherent in so many of the current weight-loss programs, led to the development of *The OC Heart Diet* Program. This plan provides access to a narrow target zone where the appropriate protein-to-carbohydrate-to-fat ratios tilt the balance of calories and macronutrients in the individual's favor.

This applies to those who want to lean-out and to those who want more energy, better endurance, improved lean-muscle mass, or improved recovery time. Surprisingly, it also serves as a great anti-aging component. This favorable balance leads to the maintenance of blood sugar levels and the balanced use of both glucose and fat for energy. Plus, the mobilization of peripheral fat stores in the adipose tissue promotes fat loss and increased energy levels.

Using the 50/25/25 low-glycemic approach allows you to reset your genetically determined set point to a new level, while simultaneously curbing hunger and cravings—something that finally makes weight loss and long-term weight maintenance a reality.

The 50/25/25 low-glycemic approach is designed to provide that precise ratio of protein and carbohydrates, coupled with the proper amount of essential fat (over 90% of Americans are deficient in this area), to create a favorable macronutrient ratio based on individual needs, meal after meal.

Furthermore, it provides a minimum of 25% of the required proteins, vitamins, and minerals necessary to maintain adequate blood levels of these critical nutrients from one meal to the next. By individualizing caloric intake, macronutrient ratios, and micronutrient intake, our program creates an environment within each individual's body that allows it to reach a new state of efficiency and economy in weight loss and weight maintenance.

Does it really work?

After all of this, the obvious question that arises is, "How do I know that the 50/25/25 approach to nutrition really works?" The first sign is a great relief from your cravings. It eliminates driving sensations of hunger due to stabilization of blood sugar levels. This is accomplished by providing you with the ideal number of calories and the best times of the day to consume them.

Ideally, this lack of hunger should be observed for three to four hours. In addition, the usual mood swings and mental fatigue associated with a drop in blood sugar levels are eliminated.

When you begin *The OC Heart Diet* Program, don't expect to see the large initial weight loss commonly associated with ketogenic diets, since most of that weight loss is water and muscle tissue—little that is permanent. However, a participant can expect to lose one to two pounds of pure fat per week. This healthy recommendation for weight loss by all the outstanding diet experts is fact. One's progress with the 50/25/25 low-glycemic approach is best determined by lack of hunger, increased energy levels, decreased body fat, and the fit of one's clothes.

14

Calculating Calorie Needs by Basal Metabolic Rate

T he basal metabolic rate (BMR) is a measure of an individu al's consumption of calories when at complete rest. It is a measure of the metabolic activity associated with involun-tary body functions such as digestion and respiration. Accurate di-rect measurement using an individual's oxygen utilization and car-bon dioxide production can be obtained in a clinical laboratory, or more recently at an office, home, or health club. Such direct mea-surements require an outlay of time and money and may not be conveniently available.

An indirect estimation of one's basal metabolic rate may be obtained using height, weight, and age. This estimate is within 10% of the measured value in most persons. More extreme vari-ance occurs in the extremely sedentary individual or in the very athletic. In those circumstances a direct measurement is neces-sary. A worksheet for calculating the basal metabolic rate is shown at the end of this chapter. Or you go to *ocheartdiet.com* for the built-in daily calculator

Daily caloric requirements

The use of an estimated *activity factor* to approximate the number of calories consumed by usual daily activity, when applied to the formula for basal metabolic rate, will provide a value for the daily consumption of calories. The formula for calculating this value using the basal metabolic rate is in the worksheet at the end of this chapter. You may also go to our web site: ocheartdiet.com to use the built in daily caloric calculator. Try to be as accurate and honest as possible in estimating your activity level!

Setting goals

In order to determine the daily caloric intake of an individualized nutrition plan, it is necessary to establish a weight-and-body composition goal. Most often the desire is to lose weight and decrease body fat, while maintaining or increasing muscle mass. The Body Mass Index (BMI) is useful, particularly if the individual is overweight. A reasonable goal is a BMI between 22 and 25. Determination of the calculated BMI will provide an incentive to remain on the individualized nutrition program.

Measurement of body-fat composition is an even more sensitive method for measuring progress. The improved accuracy and reproducibility of body-fat measurements by impedance methods has lead to the development of scales and handheld instrumentation for the measurement of body fat. The "normal" or desired level of body fat is dependent upon gender, age, and activity level, and varies within the ranges given in the appendix. See Addendum D. for references for food substitutions for additional meal plans.

Determining your Body Mass Index (BMI)

The table below indicates conversions. Find your height in the left-hand column. Move right along the top to your weight. The number indicated where these two intersect gives the BMI for your height and weight.

Body Mass Index Charts

5'0" - 5' 11" — 100 - 215 Pounds

Weight in pounds	100	105	110	115	120	125	130	135	140	145	150	155	160	165	170	175	180	185	190	195	200	205	210	215
Height																								
5'0"	19	20	21	22	23	24	25	26	27	28	29	30	31	32	33	34	35	36	37	38	39	40	41	42
5'1"	18	19	20	21	22	23	24	25	26	27	28	29	30	31	32	33	34	35	36	36	37	38	39	40
5'2"	18	19	20	21	22	22	23	24	25	26	27	28	29	30	31	32	33	33	34	35	36	37	38	39
5'3"	17	18	19	20	21	22	23	24	24	25	26	27	28	29	30	31	32	32	33	34	35	36	37	38
5'4"	17	18	18	19	20	21	22	23	24	24	25	26	27	28	29	30	31	31	32	33	34	35	36	37
5'5"	16	17	18	19	20	20	21	22	23	24	25	25	26	27	28	29	30	30	31	32	33	34	35	35
5'6"	16	17	17	18	19	20	21	21	22	23	24	25	25	26	27	28	29	29	30	31	32	33	34	34
5'7"	15	16	17	18	18	19	20	21	22	22	23	24	25	25	26	27	28	29	29	30	31	32	33	33
5'8"	15	16	16	17	18	19	19	20	21	22	22	23	24	25	25	26	27	28	28	29	30	31	32	32
5'9"	14	15	16	17	17	18	19	20	20	21	22	22	23	24	25	25	26	27	28	28	29	30	31	31
5'10"	14	15	15	16	17	18	18	19	20	20	21	22	23	23	24	25	25	26	27	28	28	29	30	30
5'11"	14	14	15	16	16	17	18	18	19	20	21	21	22	23	23	24	25	25	26	27	28	28	29	30

6'0"-6'5" — 150 - 250 Pounds

Weight in pounds	150	155	160	165	170	175	180	185	190	195	200	205	210	215	220	225	230	235	240	245	250
Height																					
6'0"	20	21	21	22	23	23	24	25	25	26	27	27	28	29	30	30	31	32	32	33	34
6'1"	19	20	21	21	22	23	23	24	25	25	26	27	27	28	29	30	30	31	32	32	33
6'2"	19	19	20	21	21	22	23	23	24	25	25	26	27	27	28	29	29	30	31	31	32
6'3"	19	19	20	20	21	22	22	23	24	24	25	25	26	27	27	28	29	29	30	30	31
6'4"	18	19	19	20	21	21	22	22	23	23	24	25	25	26	26	27	28	28	29	30	30
6'5"	17	18	19	19	20	20	21	22	22	23	23	24	25	25	26	27	27	28	28	29	29

Medical Definitions of Obesity

Medical Definitions of Obesity

Body Mass Index		Medical Definition
Women	Men	
<17.5		Anorexia
<19.5	<20.7	Underweight
19.1–25.8	20.7–26.4	In normal range (ideal weight)
25.8–27.3	26.4–27.8	Marginally overweight
27.3–32.3	27.8–31.1	Overweight
>32.3	>31.1	Very overweight or obese
35–40		Severely obese
40–50		Morbidly obese
50–60		Super obese

Reaching your target goal

Now that you have established your goals, how can the OC Diet Program help you reach them? Using your daily caloric utilization calculated from the BMR and the activity factor, you have a numeric estimate of the calories you burn each day. To lose 1 pound of fat/week, it is necessary to have a caloric deficit of approximately 600 calories/day. It is, however, unreasonable to expect that all weight loss will be body fat, and these theoretical values are further modified by the body's adaptation to a caloric deficit. However, if the daily caloric intake is between 500 and 800 calories *below* the calculated caloric intake, significant loss of body fat will occur.

Chapters 15 through 20 present sample diet plans with daily caloric intakes between 1,200 and 2,800 calories. Select a diet plan between 500 to 1,000 calories below your calculated daily caloric utilization. Sticking to this diet plan will result in an initial loss of approximately 1 pound of weight/week, of which 50 to 90 percent will be stored fat. Remember, increasing your activity level will result in more rapid fat loss.

As results become apparent, it will be necessary to recalculate your BMI, BMR, and body composition. Since a cubic inch of muscle weighs more than a cubic inch of fat, you may notice a more significant change in appearance than in weight after several months. Also, as you gain more muscle mass, your basal metabolic rate (BMR) will increase, leading to an increase in your daily caloric consumption. A good rule is to recalculate your daily caloric requirement and your diet monthly.

Exercise: A minimalist approach

Exercise is an important factor in improving health and restoring an optimal appearance. Much has been written about the value of exercise, and certainly "some is better than none." Unfortunately, many individuals cannot or will not undertake a vigorous program of structured or 'health club' exercise. For them a minimalist approach may provide the necessary incentive to engage in additional activity. Minimalist exercise requires only a pedometer and two feet. Wear a pedometer for several days and calculate the average number of steps taken daily. Exercise is described in more detail in Part III of this book.

Basal Metabolic Rate Assessment Worksheet

Name			Date

Weight/Height in Inches	Age	Sex

FINDING THE BASAL METABOLIC RATE

Use the appropriate formula for gender, then fill in weight, height, and age in the corresponding sections of the table. To calculate the resting Basal Metabolic Rate, add column A to column B, then subtract column C.

	Column A	Column B	Column C	BMR
Formula for Men	66 + (6.2 x weight in pounds)	12.7 x height in inches	6.8 x age in years	(A + B) - C = BMRExpressed as required calories per day
Formula or Women	655 + (4.4 x weight in pounds)	4.3 x height in inches	4.7 x age in years	(A + B) - C = BMR
Personal Formula	__ + (__ x__) = __ A	__ x __ = __ B	__ x __ = __ C	(__ + __)- __ A B C= __ Your BMR

Next, determine how the planned level of physical activity will impact the BMR. If physical activity goals are met, this number will accurately represent the individual metabolic rate.

Resting BMR	Activity Factor	Daily Caloric Requirement (adjusted for physical activity factor)
Resting BMR _____	1.2 for sedentary lifestyle 1.4 for moderately active lifestyle 1.6 for vigorously active lifestyle Personal Activity Factor	Resting BMR_____ x activity factor_____ = Adjusted Metabolic Rate _____

See next chapter (15) to determine your meal plan based on "Daily Caloric Requirement"

15

Dietary Plans

The following dietary plans are based on the need to lose or maintain weight. After you calculate the "Daily Caloric Re quirements" discussed in the previous chapter, choose a calorie plan based on your needs. Since all plans are based on the 50/25/25 ratio, either you will lose weight, feel great, and protect your heart, or you will maintain weight, feel great, and protect your heart. If you want to lose 1 to 2 pounds per week, choose a plan 500 to 800 calories per day less than your daily caloric requirement. Remember, if you consume 3,500 fewer calories per week than you burn up, you should lose a pound. If you feel you are at the ideal weight for you, your intake in calories should match the output. As mentioned earlier, as you gain muscle or increase your activity, over time you will need to recalculate your daily caloric needs (about once a month) until you hit a steady state.

The frequency of meals is generally five to six times per day. The reason is that smaller, more frequent meals increase your metabolism and fat burning. Whenever you eat, the body must "work" to digest the food. This increases your metabolism and increases your fat burning.

Meal-replacement shakes are available at health-food stores. You should find one that approximates the 50/25/25 carbohydrate, fat, and protein ratio. You should find one that has about 300 to 320 calories per serving; usually, this is three scoops (¾ of a cup or 75 grams would equal three scoops or one serving) or about 100 calories per scoop. For instance, when a meal plan recommends "two scoops of a meal-replacement shake," this should be about 200 calories for the shake you are using—that is, 100 calories per scoop. If the plan says four scoops, then it is 400 calories.

Please see Addendum D for reference for food substitutions for additional meal plans. Also see ocheartdiet.com for additional ideas.

1,200 Calories Per Day

Customized Meal Plan: 1200 calories per day

30 GRAMS CARBS — 15 GRAMS PROTEIN — 7 GRAMS FAT

T he following is an easy-to-follow plan for your five meals per day. Please note that you should eat 30 grams of carbo hydrates, 15 grams of protein, and 7 grams of fat at every meal. You may use only one option from each meal listed below. All amounts listed per meal will give you approximately the correct macronutrient combination and caloric count. You will also notice a meal-replacement shake, which should have a 50/25/25 carbohydrate/fat/protein ratio. Several are available at health-food stores.

Meal One Options
with Recipes

- Cinnamon Raisin Oatmeal
- 6 oz. low-fat yogurt mixed with 1½ cups cut-up fruit and a small handful of chopped almonds
- 1 egg white scrambled with 1 whole egg, ½ cup oatmeal, 1 piece fruit
- ¾ cup Healthy Choice Hi-pro cereal, ½ cup low-fat milk, 1 cup berries
- Egg White Omelet, 1 piece of whole-wheat toast with 1 tsp. butter
- Veggie Scramble, 1 piece whole-wheat toast with 2 tsp. butter, ¼ cantaloupe
- Orange French Toast
- Huevos Rancheros, ¼ cantaloupe

Cinnamon Raisin Oatmeal

½ cup cooked oatmeal
¼ tsp. cinnamon
1 packet sweetener
1 tbsp. raisins

7 almonds, chopped
½ scoop whey protein
½ cup low-fat milk

Place oatmeal in a bowl. Add cinnamon, sweetener, raisins, almonds, and protein with milk.

Scrambled Eggs with Toast

2 XL egg whites, scrambled
1 piece of sourdough toast with 1 tbsp. butter

salt and pepper to taste

Spray nonstick skillet with cooking spray. Cook eggs on medium heat until cooked to desired doneness.

Egg White Omelet

1 whole egg / 1 egg white
½ tomato, chopped
¼ onion, chopped

¼ cup mushrooms, chopped
2 oz. Parmesan cheese

In nonstick skillet, sauté onion until done. Add mushrooms and tomato. Cook slightly. Add eggs and scramble on low heat. Mix in Parmesan cheese. Serve.

Veggie Scramble

3 medium egg whites
¼ cup onion, chopped
¼ cup broccoli, chopped
¼ cup red bell peppers, chopped

¼ tomato, chopped
salt and pepper to taste
¼ tsp. garlic powder

Combine chopped vegetables in a nonstick skillet and cook. Add tomato and egg whites and scramble.

Orange French Toast

2 slices stone-ground wheat bread
¼ cup low-fat milk
2 tsp. orange extract

2 large egg whites
2 tsp. safflower oil

Mix egg whites and remaining ingredients with whisk. Dip bread into mixture. Poke holes in bread with fork to help saturate. Spray nonstick skillet with cooking spray. Place bread in skillet and then pour in rest of mixture. Cook over medium heat, turning until golden brown.

Huevos Ranchero

¼ cup tomato, chopped
[‡cup yellow bell peppers, chopped
[‡cup onion, chopped
1 corn tortilla
[‡avocado, chopped
2 XL egg whites

1 oz. asiago cheese
½ cup pinto beans
salt and pepper to taste
dried parsley
¼ tsp. garlic powder
Ranchero sauce

Set tortilla aside after warming it. Mix egg whites and vegetables together. Spray skillet with nonstick cooking spray and pour in mixture. Cook over medium heat until done. Place on warm tortilla. Pour on Ranchero sauce and sprinkle cheese over it.

Meal Two

- 2 scoops of a meal-replacement shake blended with cold water.

Meal Three Options
with Recipes

- 1 Baja Fresh grilled-fish taco served with ¾ cup black beans
- Oriental Chicken Salad (3 oz. chicken, dressing on the side)
- ½ cup cut-up fruit
- 3 oz. fajitas served with ¾ cup black beans
- Subway six-inch Roasted Chicken Breast Sandwich (add oil)
- ½ El Pollo Loco Pollo Bowl
- Tuna sandwich
- Fresh Fruit and Cottage Cheese Salad
- Turkey Avocado Wrap
- Cracker, Tuna, Avocado Stack

Tuna Sandwich

2 slices rye bread
2 tsp. mayonnaise
lettuce

2 slices tomato
2 oz. white albacore tuna

Mix tuna and mayo. Layer tuna mixture, lettuce, and tomato on bread.

Fresh Fruit and Cottage Cheese Salad

¼ cup apple, chopped
¼ cup pear, chopped
¼ cup banana, chopped
¼ cantaloupe, chopped

½ whole peach, chopped
4 oz. 2% cottage cheese
7 almonds, chopped

Mix fruit, almonds, and cottage cheese together.

Turkey Avocado Wrap

1 flour tortilla

[‡avocado, sliced

2 slices turkey

2 slices tomato

4 slices of cucumber

lettuce leaves

2 tsp. mustard

2 tbsp. low-fat yogurt

Mix mustard and yogurt. Spread over tortilla. Place avocado, tomato, cucumber, and lettuce on tortilla along with turkey. Roll into a tight tube and close one end.

Cracker, Tuna, Avocado Stack

3 high-fiber crackers

2½ oz. albacore tuna

$\frac{1}{6}$ medium avocado, sliced

1 tomato, sliced

Stack tuna, avocado, and tomato on crackers.

Meal Four

- 2 scoops of a meal-replacement shake blended with cold water.

Meal Five Options
with Recipes

- 3 oz. pork or veal (grilled), 1½ cups grilled or steamed vegetables, 1 cup of mixed berries or fruit
- 3 oz. London Broil or salmon (barbequed), 1 cup grilled or steamed vegetables, 1 small baked potato (plain)
- 3 oz. Chicken or Salmon Caesar Salad with low-fat dressing, 1 cup fruit
- Carnitas and beans
- 1 Lean Cuisine Oriental Beef
- 1 Lean Cuisine Beef Pot Roast
- Fish and vegetables with rice
- Szechwan Beef Stir Fry

Carnitas and Beans

1 corn tortilla
1 medium tomato, chopped
1 cup black beans
¼ cup red bell peppers, chopped
¼ cup onion, chopped
¼ tsp. chili powder

cilantro
2 tbsp. roasted garlic salsa
2 oz. lean beef, chopped
salt and pepper to taste
1 oz. asiago cheese

Cook beef in skillet. Add onion, red bell peppers. Cook until done. Add tomato, black beans, cilantro, and salsa. Cook over medium heat until done. Place mixture over tortilla and sprinkle with cheese.

Fish and Vegetables with Rice

2 oz. Halibut, broiled or barbequed ¼ cup sugar snap peas
¾ cup cooked rice ¼ cup celery, chopped
¼ cup zucchini, chopped salt and pepper to taste
¼ cup yellow bell peppers, chopped ¼ tsp. garlic powder
¼ cup yellow squash, chopped 2 tbsp. soy sauce
¼ cup mushrooms, sliced

Steam vegetables until *al dente*. Mix cooked fish, steamed vegetables, seasonings, soy sauce, and rice together. Place fish on side or on top.

Szechwan Beef Stir Fry

½ cup cooked brown rice 6 tsp. teriyaki sauce
2 oz. lean beef ½ cup bean sprouts
3 tsp. Szechwan sauce ¼ cup onion, chopped
1 tsp. garlic 1 tbsp. garlic, chopped
¼ cup bell pepper, chopped ¼ cup snow peas
¼ cup water chestnuts ¼ cup mushroom, sliced

Spray nonstick skillet with cooking spray and stir-fry beef, onions, bell pepper, garlic, and broccoli. when done, add bean sprouts, water chestnuts, snowpeas, mushrooms, Szechwan sauce, teriyaki sauce, and seasonings. Cook over medium heat until done. Pour over rice.

1,600 Calories per Day

Customized Meal Plan: 1,600 calories per day

40 GRAMS CARBS — 20 GRAMS PROTEIN — 9 GRAMS FAT

The following is an easy-to-follow plan for your five meals per day. Please note that you should eat 40 grams of carbo hydrates, 20 grams of protein, and 9 grams of fat at every meal. You may use one option from each meal listed below. All amounts listed per meal will give you approximately the correct macronutrient combination and caloric count.

Meal One Options

with Recipes

- 7 oz. low-fat yogurt mixed with 2 pieces cut-up fruit and a small handful of, chopped almonds
- 2 egg whites scrambled with 1 whole egg, ½cup oatmeal, 1 piece fruit
- 1 cup Healthy Choice Hi-pro cereal, ½ cup low-fat milk, 1 cup berries
- Cinnamon Raisin Oatmeal
- Scrambled Eggs with Toast
- Orange French Toast
- Garden Scramble, 1/4 cantaloupe

Cinnamon Raisin Oatmeal

1 cup cooked oatmeal
1 tbsp. raisins
1 tbsp. flax oil

1 scoop whey protein
¼ tsp. cinnamon
1 packet sweetener

Mix together cooked oatmeal, raisins, cinnamon, whey protein, sweetener, and flax oil.

Scrambled Eggs with Toast

3 egg whites, scrambled
2 pieces of sourdough toast with 1 tbsp. butter

salt and pepper to taste

Spray nonstick skillet with cooking spray. Cook eggs on medium heat until cooked to desired doneness.

Orange French Toast

2 slices sourdough bread
¼ cup low-fat milk

1 tsp. orange extract
1 egg white
      plus 2 whole eggs

Mix eggs, milk, and orange extract. Dip bread into mixture. Poke holes into bread with a fork to help saturate. Spray nonstick pan with cooking spray. Place bread into pan at medium heat. Pour in rest of mixture, turning over until golden brown.

Garden Scramble

2 large eggs plus 1 egg white
½ cup zucchini, chopped
¼ cup onion, chopped
½ cup broccoli, chopped
1 medium tomato, chopped

¼ cup mushrooms, chopped
2 oz. Parmesan cheese
1 tsp. canola oil
salt and pepper to taste

Spray skillet with nonstick cooking spray. While burner is at medium heat, add vegetables and seasonings. Cook until *al dente*. Then add eggs and Parmesan cheese and scramble together.

Meal Two

- 3 scoops of a meal-replacement shake blended with cold water.

Meal Three Options
with Recipes

- 1 Baja Fresh grilled-fish taco served with
  1 cup black beans
- 1 Subway six-inch Southwestern Chicken Sandwich
- 1 Subway six-inch sandwich (no mayo or oil)
- 1 Carl's Jr. Charbroiled BBQ Chicken Sandwich
- Oriental Chicken Salad (4 oz. chicken, dressing on the
  side), 1 cup cut-up fruit
- 4 oz. fajitas served with 1 cup black beans
- Chicken Salad Sandwich
- Turkey Sandwich
- Ham Sandwich
- Fresh Fruit and Cottage Cheese Salad
- Chopped Tuna Salad
- Tuna Cracker Stack

Chicken Sandwich

3 oz. canned chicken	1 medium tomato, sliced
2 tsp. mustard	6 slices cucumber
2 tsp. mayo	lettuce
2 slices stone-ground wheat bread	

Mix mustard, mayo, and chicken together. Spread on sandwich with tomato, cucumber, and lettuce.

Turkey Sandwich

2 slices (oz.) turkey	2 tsp. mayo
2 slices rye bread	1 medium tomato, sliced
2 tsp. mustard	lettuce

Spread mayo and mustard on bread. Layer turkey, lettuce, and tomato.

Ham Sandwich

4 slices (oz.) ham
2 slices rye bread
2 tsp. Dijon mustard

1 medium tomato, sliced
lettuce
1 slice low-fat cheddar
cheese

Spread mayo and mustard on bread. Layer ham, lettuce, tomato, and cheese.

Fresh Fruit and Cottage Cheese Salad

6 oz. low-fat cottage cheese
½ cup fresh berries
½ cup mixed fruit

1 small banana, cut up
9 almonds, chopped

Arrange fruits on a plate. Place cottage cheese in the center. Garnish with mint leaves.

Chopped Tuna Salad

2½ oz. white albacore tuna
1 cup celery, chopped
½ cup mushrooms, sliced
½ cup broccoli, chopped
1 medium tomato, chopped
4 tbsp. low-fat ranch dressing

¼ avocado, chopped
½ cup cauliflower, chopped
⅛ cup sunflower seeds
⅛ cup raisins
1 cup lettuce, chopped

Mix together all ingredients.

Tuna Cracker Stack

4 high fiber crackers
3½ oz. albacore tuna

¼ medium avocado, sliced
1 tomato, sliced

Stack tuna avocado and tomato on crackers.

Meal Four

3 scoops of a meal-replacement shake blended with cold water.

Meal Five Options
with Recipes

- 3½ ounces pork or veal (grilled), 2 cups grilled or steamed vegetables, 1½ cups mixed berries or fruit

- 3½ oz. London Broil or salmon (barbequed), 1½ cups grilled or steamed vegetables, 1 small baked potato (plain)
- Chicken Tortilla Soup
- Spanish Rice with Chicken
- Stir-fry Chicken with Snow Peas
- Chicken Veggie Pasta
- Halibut in Lemon Caper Sauce

Chicken Tortilla Soup

4 oz. cooked chicken
1 tomato, chopped
3 corn tortilla chips, crumbled

1 cup corn
2 tsp. safflower oil
½ onion, chopped

Place in saucepan and bring to boil, simmer for five minutes. Serve with tortilla chips on top.

Spanish Rice with Chicken

¼ cup salsa verde
½ cup tomato, chopped
1/8 cup onions, chopped
½ cup beans
¾ tsp. garlic powder
3 oz. chicken, chopped
½ cup red/orange bell peppers, chopped

¾ cup cooked rice
½ tsp. chili powder
hot sauce to taste
salt and pepper to taste
2 tsp. canola oil

Place chicken and oil in a skillet and cook until done. Then add chopped vegetables, garlic, onions, and spices on medium heat and cook until *al dente*. Add tomatoes and heat through. Pour over cooked rice.

Stir-fry Chicken with Snow Peas

3 oz. chicken breast
1 cup snow peas
1 cup broccoli, chopped
½ cup water chestnuts
¼ cup red peppers, chopped
½ cup mushrooms, sliced

¼ cup onions, chopped
2 tsp. soy sauce
⅛ tsp. garlic powder
2 tsp. canola oil
salt and pepper to taste
1 medium tomato, chopped

Place chicken and oil in skillet. Cook until done. Add snow peas, broccoli, water chestnuts, red peppers, and onions and cook until done. Then add mushrooms and tomato along with soy sauce and seasonings, and cook.

Chicken Veggie Pasta

½ cup cooked vermicelli

1 medium tomato, chopped
¼ cup sautéed onions
2 oz. Parmesan cheese
2 tsp. canola oil
3 oz. chicken breast, chopped

½ cup yellow squash, chopped

½ cup broccoli, chopped
salt and pepper to taste
¼ tsp garlic powder
¼ tsp Italian seasonings

Sauté onions with canola oil. Add chicken and cook until done. Steam squash and broccoli until *al dente*. Add to chicken and onions, along with tomato and spices. Place pasta into skillet, mix in Parmesan cheese and vegetables, and serve.

Halibut in Lemon Caper Sauce

3 oz. halibut
¼ cup onions finely, chopped
2 tsp. capers
1 tsp. lemon juice

⅛ cup white-wine vinegar
⅛ cup dry white wine
1 tbsp. butter
1 cup cooked brown rice

Place lemon juice, vinegar, and butter in saucepan and simmer until reduced in half. Pour over baked halibut, add capers, and place over 1 cup of cooked brown rice.

2,000 Calories per Day

Customized Meal Plan: 2,000 calories per day
50 GRAMS CARBS — 25 GRAMS PROTEIN — 11 GRAMS FAT

The following is an easy-to-follow plan for your five meals per day. Please note that you should eat 50 grams of carbohydrates, 25 grams of protein, and 11 grams of fat at every meal. You may use one option from each meal listed below. All amounts listed per meal will give you approximately the correct macronutrient combination and caloric count.

Meal One Options
with Recipes

- 1 small bagel (toasted) with 4 oz. lox, 1 tbsp. cream cheese, tomatoes, and onions
- 8 oz. low-fat yogurt mixed with 2 pieces cut-up fruit and a small handful of chopped almonds
- 3 egg whites scrambled with 1 whole egg, ¾ cup oatmeal, 1 piece fruit
- 10 oz. low-fat cottage cheese mixed with 2 cups cut-up fruit
- Garden Scramble with 1 slice stone-ground wheat bread (toasted) and 1 tsp. pure fruit preserves
- Veggie Ham Scramble, 1 slice flourless rye/wheat bread, 1 apple
- Ranchero Eggs, 1 corn tortilla, 1 cup grapes
- Cinnamon-raisin French Toast
- Apple Cinnamon Oatmeal

Garden Scramble

¼ cup onion, chopped
¼ cup broccoli, chopped
¼ cup yellow bell pepper, chopped
¼ cup yellow squash, chopped
¼ cup mushrooms, sliced

3 egg whites and
  1 whole egg
1 tsp. high-oleic
  sunflower oil
salt/pepper to taste
1/8 tsp. Italian spices
1/8 tsp. garlic powder

Place oil in a nonstick skillet. Sauté vegetables and seasonings over medium heat until done. Add eggs and scramble to desired doneness.

Veggie Ham Scramble

1 medium tomato, chopped
¼ cup bell pepper, chopped
½ medium zucchini, chopped
¼ cup mushrooms, chopped
3 egg whites
3 tsp. Parmesan cheese

1 slice deli ham, chopped
pepper & salt to taste
1/8 tsp. dried basil
1/8 tsp. paprika
1/8 tsp. garlic powder

Spray nonstick skillet with cooking oil. Sauté chopped veggies on medium heat until *al dente*. Add chopped ham, egg whites, and spices, and scramble.

Ranchero Eggs

Ingredients:
4 egg whites
2 tbls onion, chopped
¼ red pepper, chopped
¼ cup low-fat asiago cheese

pepper & salt to taste
1/8 tsp. chili powder
Tabasco sauce
¼ cup Ranchero sauce

Spray nonstick skillet with cooking oil. Sauté onion and bell pepper. Add seasonings, chese, and egg whites. Scramble until done. Place on plate and pour Ranchero sauce over.

Cinnamon-Raisin French Toast

2 slices flourless cinnamon-raisin bread

½ tsp. cinnamon   3 egg whites and 1 whole egg

1 tsp. vanilla extract   ¼ tsp. cinnamon

½ cup low-fat milk   1½ tbsp. butter

Mix egg whites, whole egg, milk, vanilla, and cinnamon. Dip bread in mixture and let soak for one minute. Spray nonstick skillet with cooking spray. Place bread pieces in large skillet and then pour in rest of mixture. Cook over medium heat, turning over until golden brown. Spread butter on French toast when done.

Apple Cinnamon Oatmeal

1 cup water   2 to 3 packets sweetener

½ cup dry oatmeal   1 tbsp. flax-seed oil

1 apple, chopped   1½ scoops vanilla-flavored whey protein powder

Cook oatmeal. Transfer cooked oatmeal to a bowl and add chopped apple, sweetener, whey protein powder, and flax-seed oil. Mix thoroughly.

Meal Two

- 3½ scoops of a meal-replacement shake blended with cold water.

Meal Three Options
with Recipes

- Baja Fresh Taco Combo
- 1 steak & 1 chicken soft taco
- 2 Baja Fresh Steak Tacos
- 1 Subway six-inch Southwestern Chicken Sandwich (no mayo)
- 1 Subway six-inch Asiago Caesar Chicken Sandwich
- 1½ Subway Roasted Chicken or Turkey Sandwiches (9 inches)
- 1 Carl's Jr. Charbroiled Chicken Sandwich Meal
- Denny's Grilled Chicken Breast, 1 side of vegetables, and 1 roll (no butter)
- 3 oz. turkey or ham on 1 slice of rye bread with ½ tbsp. mayo, mustard, and lettuce, 1 piece of fruit
- Stuffed Tomato with Tuna Salad and 4 high-fiber crackers
- Chicken Salad with 3 high-fiber crackers

Stuffed Tomato with Tuna Salad

1 cup celery	1 tsp. safflower oil
¼ cup, chopped onion	1 tsp. nonfat lemon-herb seasoning
1 tomato, chopped	pepper and salt to taste
2 tbsp. low-fat yogurt	1/8 tsp. garlic powder
3 oz. white albacore tuna	1/8 tsp. dried basil

Hollow out tomato. Drain tuna. Mix yogurt, oil, spices, celery, onion, and tomato with tuna. Stuff mixture into hollow tomato.

Chicken Salad

1 cup lettuce, chopped

½ cup celery, chopped

9 almonds, chopped

1 tomato, chopped

2 tbsp. low-fat yogurt

4 oz. chicken breast, chopped

1 tsp. lemon juice

1 tsp. safflower oil

1 tsp. Lemon-herb season-ing

¼ tsp. black pepper

Mix chicken, veggies, and yogurt with spices. Serve with or on crackers.

Meal four

- 3½ scoops of a meal-replacement shake blended with cold water.

Meal Five Options
with Recipes

- 4 oz. filet mignon (barbequed or broiled), ½ small baked potato, 1 oz. sour cream *or* 1 oz. butter, ¾ cup vegetables (steamed), 1 cup green salad with low-fat dressing
- 5 oz. salmon or chicken breast (grilled or broiled), 1 cup cooked rice, 1 cup vegetables (steamed), 1 cup berries
- Szechwan Pork over rice
- Turkey Chili with 10 soda-cracker squares
- Chicken and Mushroom Pasta with 1 cup green beans
- Taco Salad
- Dijon Filet of Fish with 2 cups steamed vegetables

Szechwan Pork

5 oz. pork tenderloin	1 cup snow peas
1 tsp. garlic	½ cup mushrooms, chopped
¼ cup onion, chopped	1 cup white rice cooked
1 tsp. canola oil	6 tsp. teriyaki sauce

Cut pork into one-inch cubes. Stir-fry pork in nonstick pan with garlic, onions, and oil until cooked. Add remaining ingredients to skillet and cook over low heat until hot. Serve over rice.

Turkey Chili

3 oz. ground turkey	1/8 tsp. black pepper
¼ cup bell peppers, chopped	¼ tsp. paprika
¼ cup onions, chopped	1 tsp. chili powder
2 tsp. canola oil	1 tbsp. cilantro
1 medium tomato, chopped	¼ tsp. garlic powder
½ cup tomato sauce	1 cup kidney beans

Sauté turkey, bell peppers, and onion in oil until done. Add remaining vegetables and spices. Simmer for thirty minutes. Add beans, heat through, and serve.

Chicken and Mushroom Pasta

3 tsp. Parmesan cheese
3 tsp. red-wine vinegar
2 tsp. canola oil
4 oz. skinless breast of chicken
1 cup mushrooms, chopped

1 cup cooked pasta
1 tsp. garlic
1 tsp. Italian seasonings
¼ tsp. black pepper

Cook pasta. Place chicken in nonstick pan and add oil. Cook until done. Add vinegar, mushrooms, and seasonings to pan and simmer until done. Place over pasta and sprinkle with Parmesan cheese.

Taco Salad

3 oz. cubed lean beef/ground beef
2 corn tortillas
1 cup lettuce, chopped
1 tomato, chopped
¼ cup onion, chopped

¼ cup cilantro
1 tsp. garlic powder
1 cup black beans
2 oz. nonfat cheddar cheese
1 tsp. chili powder

Bake tortillas in oven until crispy and set aside. Cook meat with onion & garlic powder in nonstick pan. Mix lettuce, tomato, cilantro, and cheese. Add meat. Place mixture on top of tortillas.

Dijon Filet of Fish

4 to 5 oz. fish filet
2 tbsp. low-fat yogurt
3 tsp. Dijon mustard
1 tsp. lemon juice
1 cup water chestnuts

1 tsp. olive oil
¼ tsp. paprika
¼ tsp. parsley
¼ tsp. basil

Preheat oven to 350°. Mix low-fat yogurt, olive oil, Dijon mustard, lemon juice, and spices and pour over fish filets. Cook for twenty minutes.

2,400 Calories per Day

Customized Meal Plan: 2,400 calories per day
60 GRAMS CARBS — 30 GRAMS PROTEIN — 13 GRAMS FAT

The following is an easy-to-follow plan for your five meals per day. Please note that you should eat 60 grams of carbohydrates, 30 grams of protein, and 13 grams of fat at every meal. You may use one option from each meal listed below. All amounts listed per meal will give you approximately the correct macronutrient combination and caloric count.

Meal One Options
with Recipes

- 1 bagel (toasted) with 5 oz. lox, 1 oz. cream cheese, tomatoes, and onions.
- 8 oz. low-fat fruit yogurt mixed with ½ scoop whey protein
- 4 egg whites scrambled with 1 whole egg, 1 cup oatmeal, 1 small piece fruit
- 4 egg whites scrambled, 1 cup corned-beef hash, ½ sliced melon
- 1½ cups low-fat cottage cheese mixed with 2 cups cut-up fruit
- Fajita Omelete, 1 pear, 1 peach
- Garden Scramble, 2 slices stone-ground wheat bread (toasted) with 2 tsp. pure fruit preserves
- Orange French Toast
- Cottage Cheese and Fruit with 4 high-fiber crackers
- Apple Cinnamon Oatmeal

Fajita Omelet

5 egg whites
¼ cup salsa
¼ avocado, chopped
¼ cup onion, chopped
¼ cup red bell pepper, chopped

salt and pepper to taste
1/8 tsp. garlic powder
1/8 tsp. chili powder
2 tsp. low-fat asiago cheese

Spray nonstick skillet with cooking oil. Sauté onion and bell pepper until done. Add salsa, seasonings, and egg whites, and scramble. Sprinkle with cheese, place avocado on top, and serve with 2 corn tortillas.

Garden Scramble and Toast

¼ cup onion, chopped
¼ cup broccoli, chopped
¼ cup yellow bell pepper, chopped
¼ cup yellow squash, chopped
¼ cup mushrooms, sliced

3 egg whites plus 2 whole eggs
1 tsp. high-oleic sunflower oil
salt and pepper to taste
1/8 tsp. Italian spices
1/8 tsp. garlic powder

Place oil in a nonstick skillet. Sauté vegetables and seasonings over medium heat until done. Add eggs and scramble to desired doneness.

Orange French Toast

3 slices sourdough bread
½ cup low-fat milk
2 tsp. orange extract
3 egg whites and 2 whole eggs

½ tsp. cinnamon
1 tsp. high-oleic safflower oil
1 packet sweetener

Mix milk, orange extract, eggs, and sweetener. Dip bread in mixture and let soak for one minute. Spray nonstick skillet with cooking spray. Place bread in skillet and then pour in rest of mixture. Cook over medium heat, turning when golden brown.

Cottage Cheese and Fruit

9 oz. 2% low-fat cottage cheese   1 tbsp. Flax-seed oil
2 cups mixed berries/fruit

Mix cottage cheese, berries/fruit, and oil.

Apple Cinnamon Oatmeal

1½ cups cooked oatmeal   1 tbsp. high-oleic sunflower oil
¼ tsp. cinnamon   2 packets sweetener
1 apple, chopped   1½ scoops whey protein powder

Mix cooked oatmeal, apple, cinnamon, sweetener, and whey protein.

Meal Two

- 4 scoops of a meal-replacement shake blended with cold water.

Meal Three Options
with Recipes

- 2 Baja Fresh, La Salsa, or Rubio's fish or chicken soft tacos
- Subway 12-inch Roasted Chicken Sandwich with oil and mayo
- 3 Baja Fresh Steak Tacos
- 1 El Pollo Loco Pollo Bowl
- 5 oz. cooked chicken breast on 2 slices flourless bread with sliced tomato, sliced cucumber, sliced avocado, lettuce, and mustard, 1 piece fruit
- 5 oz. chicken or salmon served over 2 cups salad greens with low-fat dressing, 2 whole-wheat rolls
- 4 oz. turkey or ham on 2 slices of rye bread with 1 tbsp. mayo, mustard, and lettuce
- 5 high-fiber crackers, 3 slices deli-style turkey (about 3.5 oz), sliced avocado, sliced tomato (stack on crackers)
- Turkey Avocado Sandwich with ¾ cup grapes

Turkey Avocado Sandwich with Fruit

2 slices rye bread   2 tsp. mustard
¼ avocado, sliced   lettuce
1 tomato, sliced   2 tbsp. low-fat yogurt
3 slices deli-style turkey (about 3.5 oz.)

Mix low-fat yogurt and mustard. Spread on both slices of bread. Layer lettuce, tomato, avocado, and turkey on bread.

Meal Four

- 4 scoops a meal-replacement shake blended with cold water.

Meal Five Options
with Recipes

- 5 oz. filet mignon (barbequed or broiled), 1 small baked potato, 1 oz. sour cream _or_ 1 oz. butter, ¾ cup vegetables (steamed), 1 cup green salad with low-fat dressing
- 6 oz. salmon or chicken breast (grilled or broiled), 1½ cups cooked rice, 1½ cups vegetables (steamed), 1 cup berries
- Chicken Fajita with black beans, rice, salsa, and tortilla
- Chicken Stroganoff
- Beef Vegetable Soup
- Salmon with Couscous
- Shrimp & Vegetable Stir-fry
- Turkey Chili with 15 squares soda crackers

Chicken Fajita

5 oz fish or chicken	¼ onion, sliced
½ cup rice with seasonings	salsa
¾ cup black beans (pinto or kidney)	1 flour tortilla
1 cup, sliced bell peppers (red, yellow, green)	

Sauté chicken or fish over medium heat. Add peppers and onions. Cook until done. Wrap in tortilla. Serve with beans, rice, and salsa.

Chicken Stroganoff

¾ cup cooked fettuccini	½ cup mushrooms, sliced
5 oz. chicken breast, chopped	¼ tsp. garlic powder
5 tbsp. half and half	salt and pepper to taste
3 oz. Parmesan cheese	1/8 tsp. dried basil
¼ cup onion, chopped	1/8 cup fresh parsley

Sauté onion and mushroom in nonstick skillet. Add half and half, seasonings, and Parmesan cheese, and cook over medium heat until blended and hot. Place cooked pasta in mixture. Toss and serve.

Beef Vegetable Soup

2 cup beef stock
½ cup celery, chopped
¼ cup onion, chopped
¼ cup carrots, chopped
¼ cup zucchini, chopped
¼ cup yellow squash, chopped
¼ cup red bell peppers, chopped

1 tomato, chopped
1/8 tsp. oregano
salt and pepper to taste
¼ tsp. garlic powder
1 tsp. Worcestershire sauce
4 oz. lean beef
1 cup cooked rice

Sauté beef in nonstick skillet; set aside. Put beef stock, vegetables, and seasonings in large saucepan and simmer on low heat until all vegetables are tender. Add cooked rice and beef. Heat through and serve.

Salmon with Couscous

1¼ cups cooked couscous
6 oz. salmon filet
¼ cup onion, chopped
1 tbsp. garlic, chopped

1 medium tomato, chopped
2 tbsp. half and half
1 tbsp. fresh dill

Bake salmon in 350° oven for about fifteen to twenty minutes. Sauté onion and garlic until tender. Add tomato, half and half, dill, and heat through. Place baked salmon on cooked couscous and pour sauce over top.

Shrimp & Vegetable Stir-fry

6 oz. large shrimp
¼ cup broccoli, chopped
¼ cup mushrooms, sliced
¼ cup water chestnuts
½ cup bean sprouts
¼ cup onion, chopped
¼ cup yellow squash, chopped

¼ cup red bell pepper, chopped
1 tsp. crushed garlic
1 tbsp. sunflower oil
1 tbsp. soy sauce (or to taste)
salt and pepper to taste
1 cup cooked brown or
   wild rice

Place sunflower oil in nonstick skillet and stir-fry shrimp over medium heat until almost done. Add remaining ingredients and stir-fry on medium heat until done (about seven to nine minutes). Serve over rice.

Turkey Chili

4 oz. lean ground turkey
1 tomato, chopped
¼ cup bell peppers, chopped
¼ cup onions, chopped
¼ cup mushrooms, chopped
1 cup canned beans (kidney, black, pinto, etc.)

½ tsp. chili powder
1 tbsp. tomatillo sauce
¼ cup salsa verde
¼ tsp. garlic powder
salt and pepper to taste

Sauté turkey, bell peppers, and onion until done. Add mushrooms, tomatoes, beans, salsa, tomatillo sauce, and spices. Simmer for thirty minutes. Add beans, heat through, and serve.

2,800 Calories Per Day

Customized Meal Plan: 2,800 calories per day
70 GRAMS CARBS — 35 GRAMS PROTEIN — 15 GRAMS FAT

T he following is an easy-to-follow plan for your five meals per day. Please note that you should eat 70 grams of carbo hydrates, 35 grams of protein, and 15 grams of fat at every meal. You may use one option from each meal listed below. All amounts listed per meal will give you approximately the correct macronutrient combination and caloric count.

Meal One Options
with Recipes

- 1½ bagels (toasted) with 6 oz. lox, 1 oz. cream cheese, tomatoes, and onions
- 12 oz. low-fat fruit yogurt mixed with 1 scoop whey protein
- 5 egg whites scrambled with 1 whole egg, 1 cup oatmeal, 1 piece fruit
- 3 egg whites scrambled, 1 cup corned-beef hash, ½ sliced melon
- 1¾ cups low-fat cottage cheese mixed with 2 cups cut-up fruit
- Scrambled Eggs and Toast, 1 banana
- Cinnamon-raisin French Toast
- Apple Cinnamon Oatmeal
- Eggs Ranchero with 2 corn tortillas and 1 cup berries

Scrambled Eggs and Toast

6 egg whites
1 tsp. high-oleic sunflower oil
salt and pepper to taste

2 slices sourdough toast
1 pat butter

Add 1 tsp. high-oleic sunflower oil to nonstick skillet. Over medium heat add egg whites and seasonings. Scramble to desired doneness. Put butter on the two slices of sourdough toast.

Cinnamon-raisin French Toast

4 slices stone-ground wheat bread
6 egg whites
½ cup low-fat milk
½ tsp. cinnamon

1 packet sweetener
1 oz. raisins
1½ tbsp. butter

Mix egg whites, milk, cinnamon, and sweetener. Dip bread in mixture and let soak for one minute. Spray nonstick skillet with cooking spray. Place bread pieces in large skillet and then pour in rest of mixture. Sprinkle in raisins. Cook over medium heat, turning until golden brown. Spread butter on French toast when done.

Apple Cinnamon Oatmeal

2 cups water
1 cup dry oatmeal
1 apple, chopped

2 to 3 packets sweetener
1½ tbsp. Flax-seed oil
2 scoops vanilla-flavored
    whey protein powder

Cook oatmeal. Transfer cooked oatmeal to a bowl and add chopped apple, sweetener, whey protein powder, and flax-seed oil. Mix thoroughly.

Eggs Ranchero

6 egg whites
1/8 cup onion, chopped
1/4 cup asiago cheese
1/4 red pepper, chopped
Tabasco sauce

1/2 cup Ranchero sauce
1/4 tsp. garlic powder
salt and pepper to taste
1/8 tsp. chili powder

Spray nonstick skillet with cooking oil. Sauté onion and bell pepper. Add seasonings, cheese, and egg whites. Scramble until done. Place on plate and pour Ranchero sauce over.

Meal Two

- 5 scoops of a meal-replacement shake blended with cold water.

Meal Three Options
with Recipes

- Subway 12-inch Turkey Sandwich with everything on it
- 1 steak and 2 chicken Baja Fresh, La Salsa, or Rubio's soft tacos
- 1 cooked chicken breast cut up in 2 cups of cooked rice and 1½ cups steamed veggies
- 6 oz. cooked chicken breast on 2 slices flourless bread with sliced tomato, sliced cucumber, sliced avocado, lettuce, and mustard, plus 1 piece fruit
- 6 oz. chicken or salmon served over 2 cups salad greens with low-fat dressing, plus 2 whole-wheat rolls
- 5 oz. turkey or ham on 2 slices of rye bread with 1 tbsp. mayo, mustard, and lettuce.
- Cracker Turkey Stack
- Turkey and Cheese Lettuce Wrap, plus 1 sliced papaya and 1 oat-bran muffin
- Tuna Sandwich and ¼ honeydew melon
- Salmon Salad with 2 sourdough rolls

Cracker Turkey Stack

6 high-fiber crackers	1-slice avocado
1-slice tomato	3-slices deli-style turkey (about 4 oz.)

Stack turkey, sliced avocado, and sliced tomato on crackers.

Turkey and Cheese Lettuce Wrap

3½ oz. sliced turkey	1 tomato, chopped
4 large lettuce leaves	1 tbsp. low-fat mayo
2 slices Swiss cheese	1 tsp. lemon-herb seasoning
¼ cup onions, chopped	salt and pepper to taste

Combine mayo, chopped tomato, onion, spices, and seasonings. Place turkey with mayo mixture in center of lettuce leaves. Put Swiss cheese on top and fold edges of lettuce together like a burrito.

Tuna Sandwich

5 oz. white albacore tuna
2 tbsp. low-fat mayo
1 tomato, chopped
¼ cup celery, chopped

Romaine lettuce leaves
salt and pepper to taste
2 slices rye bread

Mix mayo, tomato, celery, and seasonings. Add tuna and mix thoroughly. Place lettuce leaves on bread and add tuna mixture.

Salmon Salad

6 oz. salmon
2 cups lettuce, chopped
¼ cup mushrooms .
¼ onion, sliced
1 tomato, chopped

½ cucumber, chopped
½ yellow pepper, chopped
1 zucchini, chopped
¼ tsp. garlic powder
salt and pepper to taste

Dressing

¼ cup balsamic vinegar
2 tsp. sesame oil

½ tsp. soy sauce
1⁄8 tsp. dill

Mix ingredients together, pour dressing over salad, and toss.

Meal Four

- 5 scoops of a meal-replacement shake blended with cold water.

Meal Five Options
with Recipes

- 6 oz. filet mignon (barbequed or broiled), 1 small baked potato, 1 oz. sour cream <u>or</u> 1 oz. butter, 1 cup vegetables (steamed), 1 cup green salad with low-fat dressing
- 6 oz. salmon or chicken breast (grilled or broiled), 1½ cups cooked rice, 2 cups vegetables (steamed), 1 cup berries
- Chicken or Steak Fajitas with beans, rice, salsa, and tortillas
- Chicken Mushroom Pasta
- Braised Lamb with 1 sourdough roll and 2 cups berries
- Orange Roughy
- Stir-fry Chicken with snow peas, plus 1 cup mixed fruit and 1 slice banana bread
- Dijon Filet of Fish with 2 cups mixed squashes (steamed), 2 sourdough rolls, 1 cup mixed berries

Chicken or Steak Fajitas

6 oz. steak or chicken ½ cup rice with seasonings
¼ onion, sliced salsa
¾ cup black beans (pinto or kidney) 2 flour tortillas
1 cup sliced bell peppers (red, yellow, green)

Sauté meat or fish over medium heat. Add peppers and onions. Cook until done. Wrap in tortillas. Serve with beans, rice, and salsa.

Chicken Mushroom Pasta

6 oz. chicken breast cut into one-inch cubes

1-cup mushrooms, chopped	¼ tsp. paprika
1 medium tomato, chopped	¼ tsp. Italian herbs
4 oz. Parmesan cheese	¼ tsp. garlic powder
¼ cup low-fat milk	¼ tsp. onion powder
⅛ tsp. black pepper	1 tbsp. cornstarch
¼ tsp. parsley	1 cup macaroni

Cook cubes of chicken in a nonstick skillet until well done. In a saucepan put mushrooms, tomato, Parmesan cheese, low-fat milk, seasonings, and cornstarch, and cook over medium heat until a creamy sauce is formed. Cook macaroni until *al dente*. Place macaroni in a bowl. Place chicken over it and add sauce. Mix together thoroughly.

Braised Lamb

5 oz. boneless lamb, chopped	1 tsp. garlic powder
2 cups celery, chopped	¼ tsp. black pepper
½ cup onions, chopped	¼ tsp. dried basil
1 cup tomato puree	salt to taste

Spray nonstick skillet with cooking oil. Add lamb to skillet and cook until well done. Add chopped vegetables, seasonings, and remaining ingredients. Cover and simmer over low heat until done.

Orange Roughy

8 oz. Orange Roughy or Filet of Sole

½ cup mandarin oranges	4 tbsp. raisins
6 tbsp. low-fat yogurt	¼ tsp. curry powder
2 tsp. lemon juice	1 tsp. safflower oil mixed

with black pepper, chopped basil, and chopped parsley

Rub fish with oil mixture. Mix oranges, raisins, lemon juice, and yogurt. Put fish in baking pan and pour yogurt mixture over. Bake at 350° for twenty minutes.

Stir-fry Chicken with Snow Peas

6 oz. chicken breast, cubed
1 cup mushrooms, sliced
1 cup snow peas
½ cup garbanzo beans
1 medium tomato, chopped
½ cup onion, chopped
1 tbsp. garlic, chopped

½ cup celery, chopped
½ cup carrots, chopped
1 yellow bell pepper, chopped
2 tbsp. soy sauce
1 tbsp. peanut oil
¼ tsp. dried ginger
½ cup water chestnuts

Spray nonstick wok with cooking oil. Place peanut oil and cubed chicken into wok and cook until done. Add onion, garlic, water chestnuts, bell pepper, celery, and carrots, and cook until *al dente*. Add mushrooms, snow peas, garbanzo beans, tomato, along with soy sauce and dried ginger and cook until done.

Dijon Filet of Fish

5 oz. Halibut
¼ cup low-fat yogurt
2 tsp. Dijon mustard
1 tsp. sugar
1 tsp. lemon juice
2 tsp. sesame oil

¼ tsp. dried parsley
¼ tsp. dried dill
¼ tsp. garlic powder
¼ tsp. onion powder
salt and pepper to taste

Broil halibut until tender. Mix yogurt, mustard, sugar, lemon juice, sesame oil, and seasonings together. Heat in saucepan over low heat until hot. *Do not overheat or allow to boil.* Pour sauce over halibut.

Vegan Customized Meal Plan

Customized Meal Plan: 1,600 calories per day

40 GRAMS CARBS — 20 GRAMS PROTEIN — 9 GRAMS FAT

Vegan/Fish/Chicken Choice

Y ou may use one option from each meal listed below. All amounts listed per meal will give you approximately the correct macronutrient combination and caloric count.

Meal One Options

- 6 ounces low-fat yogurt, 2 pieces fruit, 6 almonds
- 4 egg whites, 1 cup oatmeal, 1 piece fruit, 1 slice bread

- 1 whole egg, 1 piece fruit, 1 scoop whey
- 6 oz. 2% cottage cheese, 2 pieces fruit (cut up)
- 1 cup oatmeal, 1 piece fruit, 4 egg whites
- 1 cup Hi-pro cereal, 2 oz. flax meal, 1 piece fruit

Meal Two

- 1 scoop meal-replacement shake in water *or* 1 meal-replacement bar *or* ¾ Naked Juice Pro Plus

Meal Three Options

- tuna-salad sandwich, 1 tbsp. mayo, tomato, onions, lettuce, bread
- 1 veggie burger
- 1 cup beans w/ salsa
- 5 oz. tofu and 2 pieces fruit
- 5 oz. tofu, ½ cup rice
- 6-inch Subway Tuna w/ everything
- Salad w/ ½ avocado, 5 oz. tofu, nuts, broccoli, legumes, celery, apples, raisins, etc., nonfat dressing

Meal Four

- 1 scoop meal-replacement powder *or* 1 meal-replacement bar *or* ¾ Naked Juice Pro Plus

Meal Five Options

- 3 oz. fish, ½ cup beans, ¾ cup rice, onions, red, green, & yellow, peppers, seasoning
- 3 oz. seafood,, grilled, ¾ cup pasta, vegetarian sauce, miso soup, veggies, ½ cup berries
- Seafood or veggie burger w/seasonings, 2 cups veggies, ¾ cup rice
- 5 oz. tofu w/¾ cup rice, veggies, seasonings

Vegan Customized Meal Plan

Customized Meal Plan: 2,000 calories per day

50 GRAMS CARBS — 25 GRAMS PROTEIN — 11 GRAMS FAT

Vegan/Eggs Choice

Meal One

- 10 oz. low-fat yogurt, 2 pieces fruit, 6 almonds
- 2 egg whites, 2 whole eggs, 2 pieces fruit
- 1 cup oatmeal, 1 piece fruit, 1.5 scoops whey
- 1 cup oatmeal, 1.5 scoops Whey Pro, 1 piece fruit
- 2 egg whites, 2 pieces fruit 1 tbsp. flax oil
- 7 oz. 2% cottage cheese, 2 pieces fruit (cut up)
- 2 whole eggs, 4 oz. fruit juice

Meal Two

- 1.5 scoops meal-replacement shake in water <u>or</u> 1 Promax meal-replacement bar <u>or</u> One Naked Juice Pro Plus

Meal Three

- Shrimp-salad sandwich, 6 oz. tofu and, 2 pieces fruit
- 1 veggie burger, 1 tbsp. mayo, tomato, onions, lettuce, 2 slices bread
- 1 cup beans w/ 6 oz. tofu, ½ cup rice, salsa
- Shrimp salad w/ everything
- Salad w/ ½ avocado, 6 oz. tofu, nuts, broccoli, legumes, celery, apples, raisins, etc., nonfat dressing

Meal Four

- 1.5 scoops meal-replacement powder *or* 1 Promax meal-replacement bar *or* One Naked Juice Pro Plus

Meal Five

- 4 oz. shrimp, veggies, ½ cup berries
- 6 oz. tofu, ½ cup beans, ¾ cup rice, onions,
- 4 oz. seafood, ½ cup pasta, vegetarian sauce
- Veggie burger, red, green, yellow peppers w/seasonings,
- 4 oz. grilled prawns, 2 cups veggies w/seasonings, 1 cup rice
- 6 oz. tofu, ¾ cup rice, veggies w/seasonings
- 7 oz. low-fat cottage cheese w/ 6 small red potatoes & veggies

16

Vitamins and Supplements
The Bottom Line

B illions of dollars are spent each year on a magic pill—a magic supplement to wipe away heart disease, cancer, and other maladies of modern life. The problem is, there is no magic pill. Scientific evidence, even when favorable for vitamins and supplements, points to modest benefits at best. The following are our evaluations and recommendations for various vitamins and supplements in regard to their benefit (or lack thereof) in preventing or treating heart disease.

Vitamins

Vitamin A (beta carotene)
No benefit seen.

Vitamin E
No benefit seen. Similar outcome as vitamin C when combined with statins. If you need to take vitamin E, limit the dose to 400 iu per day.

Vitamin C

No benefit seen. One study showed an adverse effect in patients taking statins alone versus patients taking statins plus vitamins C and E. Those who took the vitamins had more cardiac events than those taking the statin alone. If you need to take vitamin C over the long run, limit it to 500 mg or less per day. This non benefit for vitamin C has also been demonstrated in a recent study using EBCT scans.

Vitamin B3 (niacin)

Niacin at the proper doses is one of most effective medications to raise HDL cholesterol, change the LDL particle size to the less-dangerous larger particle size, lower LDL and triglyceride levels, and lower the levels of the potentially dangerous Lipoprotein (a) [Lp (a)]. The doses required are at least 500 to 1,000 mg per day, often up to 3,000 mg per day. These doses require physician supervision due to possible liver inflammation.

Vitamin B_6 (pyridoxine)

Pyridoxine has been shown to reduce the chance of arteries re-narrowing after PTCA when combined with folic acid and vitamin B_{12}. These three B vitamins all help reduce homocysteine levels. High doses of pyridoxine can be toxic. 50 mg per day of pyridoxine is reasonable after PTCA/stents or for high homocysteine levels.

Vitamin B_{12}

Provides a complementary effect to folic acid and pyridoxine in treating high homocysteine levels. 1,000 micrograms per day is reasonable.

Folic Acid

Provides a complementary effect on lowering homocysteine levels with the other B vitamins. 400 to 1,000 mcg per day is reasonable. Almost all multivitamins have 400 mcg of folic acid.

Supplements

Aspirin

Any man or woman with coronary calcium should take at least 81 mg per day of aspirin. There has recently been a lot of discussion about some people being "aspirin resistant", meaning they need high doses of aspirin to get heart-protecting benefits. It is not clear at this time, if anyone, needs to be tested for aspirin resistance. There is some evidence that if you take NSAIDs (non-steroidal anti-inflammatory drugs) like ibuprofen, naproxen, Vioxx, Celebrex, and others, you probably should take 325 mg of aspirin per day, since NSAID counteract the anti-clotting effects of aspirin.

Coenzyme Q10

There is weak evidence that it may benefit patients with congestive heart failure and patients who are taking statins. In both situations lower levels of Q10 are seen. 50 mg per day is reasonable, up to 180mg per day. It is also helpful in preventing muscle aches from statins. However, muscle aches should first be reported to the physician.

Cholestin

Red-rice yeast is a weak natural form of lovastatin. (The first available statin was the Mevacor brand of lovastatin). Red-rice yeast appears to be effective in lowering cholesterol. There is some question about the consistency and purity of the preparations. It may be cheaper than the commercially available statins, but when used to bring cholesterol levels down to similar levels, the price benefit may vanish.

Garlic

There is weak evidence that it may lower cholesterol, blood pressure, and homocysteine levels, as well as reduce clot formation. Aged garlic extract is probably the most effective. Most effective dose not yet determined.

Gugulipid (guggalgum)
Conflicting studies, but probably effective in lowering cholesterol: About 75 mg per day.

Hawthorn
May have some benefit in patients with congestive heart failure. The effects are somewhat similar to the popular ACE inhibitor class of blood-pressure medications that dilate the blood vessels and are also helpful in congestive heart failure. Most effective dose not known.

Policosanol
Policosanol is a mixture from sugar cane or rice-bran wax. It inhibits the production of cholesterol and lowers total cholesterol and LDL(about31%) as well as raises HDL(about 25%). Effective dose about 10 to 20 mg per day.

Fish Oil and **Flax Seed Oil**
Both contain omega-3 fatty acids, which have triglyceride-lowering properties, and anti-inflammatory and anti-clotting properties. The omega-3 fatty acids are similar to those found in cold-water fish like salmon, mackerel, and tuna. Dose of 3,000 to 6,000 mg per day if you do not respond to the usual dietary measures to reduce triglycerides.

Food Supplements

Oat Bran and Barley

Both been shown to lower cholesterol and are two of the four foods approved by the FDA (almonds and soy are the other two foods) to state that they do lower cholesterol. Eat about ¼ cup per day. The mechanism is that oat bran and barley inhibit the absorption of cholesterol from the intestine (similar to psyllium in Metamucil).

Nuts

Nut have been shown to lower cholesterol. About ½ cup per day of raw nuts is reasonable, but they are very dense in calories. Almonds, walnuts, and pecans appear to be the most effective. The mechanism is not clear, but they most likely inhibit cholesterol production by the liver and cholesterol absorption in the intestine.

Olive Oil

Olive oil has been shown to reduce the risk of heart disease when people replace foods with high concentrations of saturated fat, with the monounsaturated fat in olive oil. The FDA recently gave approval for food labeling on olive oil to indicate such a benefit. Evidence suggests eating two tablespoons of olive oil per day may reduce the risk of coronary artery heart disease. The mainstays of the Mediterranean diet are foods high in unsaturated fats, olive oil and other vegetable oils, nuts and fish as tuna and salmon.

Soy Protein

Soy protein can lower total cholesterol and LDL cholesterol about 10%, though some recent studies cast some doubt. Usually, about 20 to 25 gm of soy protein per day is needed, which is the equivalent to about two and one-half cups of soymilk.

Margarines That Lower Cholesterol

Benecol® and Take Control® are plant-derived margarines that inhibit cholesterol absorption in the intestine. About a 7 percent LDL reduction can occur if a 1 gm serving is used each day.

Caffeine

There are no conclusive benefits to caffeine in regards to the heart. Two to four cups of a beverage containing caffeine is safe as long as you are not sensitive to the potential side effects which usually are irregular heart beats, often felt as palpitations, or a fluttering or a skipped beat sensation. If these occur you are wise to stop all caffeine intake. Coffee that is not filtered has more oils than filtered coffee and in some individuals may change cholesterol levels to a slight degree. Tea, especially green tea may have benefits independent of caffeine. The bottom line is coffee and tea are generally safe to take in moderation and there may be some health benefits to green tea.

Special Foods

Alcohol

Two drinks per day for a man and one drink per day for a woman have shown benefit in protecting from heart disease. One drink is considered to be twelve ounces of beer, one ounce of whiskey or four ounces of wine. A recent study using EBCT scans showed less extensive coronary calcification in those who drank two or less drinks per day. However, remember that alcohol has 7 calories per gram, carbohydrates have 4 calories per gram, and fats have 9 calories per gram. Alcohol is not only calorie dense, but it suppresses fat burning leading to a greater amount of the calories being stored as fat, especially in the abdomen (the more dangerous visceral fat). However, unless you enjoy alcohol, it probably is not worthwhile making alcohol a part of your heart-protection regimen.

Eggs

Eggs have fallen in an out of favor over the past several decades. Eggs are considered the near perfect food. However, three decades ago, when it was discovered that cholesterol caused heart disease, it was then thought that the 213 mg of cholesterol in each egg would be unhealthy for your heart. We now know that eating cholesterol has only a mild effect on blood cholesterol levels. Eating saturated fat and trans-fatty acids are the main foods that cause elevated blood cholesterol. Studies show that one egg per day (not fried) does not contribute to heart disease.

Shellfish

Shellfish have cholesterol which has caused the misconception that shellfish are unhealthy. But, like the cholesterol in eggs, there is no adverse cardiovascular effects from eating shellfish. Shellfish, like other fish are very beneficial to heart health.

Milk

Milk is a nutritious food. Numerous studies report conflicting results between milk intake and heart disease, A recent British study that followed milk drinkers over 20 years did not show an increase in heart disease in milk drinkers, However, if you want to drink milk, a reasonable approach would be to drink non-fat milk or low fat milk if you have elevated cholesterol or coronary calcification until studies are more definitive as to the risk.

Amino Acid Supplements

L-arginine

An amino acid with unique properties, L-arginine contributes to the production of nitrous oxide in the inner lining of arteries called the endothelium. The endothelium lines the inner surface of the arteries and produces nitrous oxide, which then causes the artery to relax and dilate. When this is done in the coronary arteries, it increases blood flow to the heart and can help relieve angina. Blood pressure may also decrease due to dilatation of the larger blood vessels in the arms and legs. There is growing evidence that it may also inhibit plaque formation by inhibiting inflammation and injury to the endothelium.

The exact dose is unknown but somewhere between 1,000 to 6,000 mg per day in two divided doses. In some susceptible people, it may cause a flare-up of herpes or shingles. Gastrointestinal upset and diarrhea may also occur. L-arginine may also help with erectile dysfunction in a manner similar to Viagra, which also works by increasing nitrous-oxide production in the arteries. Recent studies suggest that L-arginine should not be given to patients during a heart attack. Taking L-arginine after a heart attack is probably alright to do.

L-carnitine
An amino acid that can lower cholesterol and lipoprotein (a) [also referred to as Lp (a)], thus preventing plaque formation. Exact doses are unknown, but 1,000 to 2,000 mg per day is reasonable. Sometimes mild stomach upset may occur.

Mineral Supplements

Magnesium
Magnesium is an important mineral that regulates the electrical activity of the heart. A recent study showed that magnesium plays a significant role in the fat metabolism in the walls of the coronary arteries. EBCT scans showed more calcium in the coronary arteries in those patients with a low intake of magnesium. Doses up to 500 mg per day may be beneficial in reducing irregular heart beats. However, doses this high should be under the recommendation of a physician for two reasons. First, the cause of irregular heart beats needs to be determined. Second, magnesium is excreted through the kidneys into the urine. If you have some underlying kidney disease, the magnesium could build up in the bloodstream to toxic levels.

Protein supplements

Not all protein is the same. Whey protein and egg whites are the best absorbed and utilized proteins. Soy is a close second and has additional cholesterol-lowering benefits. If you are going to use a meal-replacement shake, it should contain whey protein or soy protein.

Hormone replacement

Hormone replacement is still very controversial. From a cardiology perspective, the following are reasonable from what we know now:

Testosterone replacement for men

Probably beneficial overall to restore testosterone levels near high normal. Supernormal levels, however, may drop HDL levels and promote heart disease. Our recent study at the Orange County Heart Institute, using EBT scanning for coronary calcium in professional bodybuilders, showed severe coronary calcification (hardening of the arteries) in the majority of the bodybuilders we studied. They all had very low HDL (<10). It is not clear if high doses of steroids have a direct toxic effect on the lining of the coronary arteries or an indirect effect due to extremely low HDL levels.

Estrogen/Progesterone replacement in women

The bottom line is that estrogen is beneficial for the heart when given without accompanying progesterone. Estrogen raises HDL, lowers total cholesterol and helps keep arteries pliable. A recent study using EBCT scans showed less coronary calcification in women on estrogen replacement (without the addition of progesterone). If severe menopausal symptoms are present, hormone replacement is reasonable if not within a timeframe of one to two years after a recent heart attack. We no longer prescribe hormone replacement to women just for its heart-protection and cholesterol benefits.

Summary

A reasonable approach to using supplements to maintain a heart healthy lifestyle would be to take the following on a daily basis: a multivitamin with the addition of vitamins B_6, B_{12}, 1,000mg of fish oil and 81 mg of aspirin. Use margarines that lower cholesterol as a butter or margarine substitute, and add a glass of soymilk per day (if you like the taste). Take a statin and/or niacin or a fibrate based on your coronary calcium score and your cholesterol profile as discussed earlier in this book (under the direction of your physician).

Though the above supplements have some cholesterol-lowering benefits, if you have high coronary calcium scores (e.g., above 100), you really need statins and/or niacin or fibrates, since these products have been extensively studied to not only lower cholesterol but also to prevent cardiac events. Most supplements have not undergone such extensive testing in rigid clinical trials, following tens of thousands of patients to see if cardiac events were prevented.

Lowering cholesterol alone may not prevent cardiac events, since statins also have anti-inflammatory properties and plaque-stabilizing properties not found in all cholesterol-lowering supplements. When your calcium score is over 100, you absolutely need a scientifically proven approach.

If you do not have coronary calcium on EBT scanning and your cholesterol is high, it is reasonable to try to take policosanol, gugulipid, cholestin, garlic, soy, and oat and bran cereal to lower cholesterol. Fish and flax oil would be best for high triglycerides. L-arginine (1,000mg to 6,000mg per day) and L-carnitine (1,000mg to 2,000mg per day) would be reasonable if plaque is present.

Part III

Physical activity is a crucial part of the battle against heart disease. Proper nutrition when combined with exercise, greatly magnify the benefit of each other. *The OC Heart Diet* is an integrated plan of proper foods in correct proportions, that when combined with exercise gives greater balance to your weight loss and life-long energy needs. You will discover there are methods of exercise that work and require less physical stress for maximum results. You can start with the simplest of programs and in no time find yourself in good enough condition to move about with ease. *The OC Heart Diet* and Fitness Program include a workable cardiovascular exercise routine that will work for you.

17

Exercise
and
The OC Heart Diet

Exercise is the center point of *The OC Heart Diet*. Dietary changes alone will benefit your heart, but for the very maximum benefit, this lifestyle program requires exercise. Key to *The OC Heart Diet* program is *aerobic exercise and weight training* (also called resistance training or strength training) with proper intake of *carbohydrates, protein, and fats!* Effective muscle strength and toning cannot be obtained without proper carbohydrate intake as outlined in the diet section of this book. Exercise makes your heart stronger by helping to pump more blood with each beat. Blood delivers more oxygen to your body, which helps it function more efficiently. Exercise can also lower blood pressure. In fact, about thirty percent of those with high blood pressure can control their blood pressure with proper exercise. Exercise can reduce levels of LDL ("bad" cholesterol) that clogs the arteries and can cause a heart attack. Exercise can also raise levels of HDL ("good" cholesterol), which helps protect against heart disease. In fact, exercise is the most effective way to raise HDL. Exercise reduces the clotting potential of your blood, prevents wide swings in harmful adrenaline levels in your blood, helps control blood sugar, prevents osteoporosis and exercise an also help elevate your mood.

Combined with a healthy diet, exercise can speed up weight loss. Exercise is also the best way to maintain weight loss. Regular exercise also helps you burn calories faster, even when you're sitting still! No single medicine can do for your heart what regular exercise can do. *Exercise is the most effective pill for protecting your heart.*

Understanding muscle function

Muscles use carbohydrates, fats, and protein as energy sources. Carbohydrates are the preferred sources of energy for muscle contraction. Depending on the intensity and duration of exercise, muscles use all three energy sources in some proportion. Obviously, it is least desirable when muscles use protein as an energy source rather than for muscle building. It is most desirable when fats are the predominant energy source during your exercise. Muscles prefer to use protein for muscle repair and building. Fats are the preferred stored-energy source, and carbohydrates are the usual energy source for contracting muscle fibers.

Carbohydrates are stored in the body in the form of glycogen in the muscles and the liver. Glycogen is broken down into glucose to be used for energy. Also, carbohydrates in the digestive system are used for glucose sources. Glycogen is consumed during bursts of anaerobic activity, like sprinting, when adequate oxygen is not available for use during bursts of exercise. Lactic acid is produced, which shortly limits the activity. Fats require adequate oxygen in order to be used as energy. Glycogen becomes depleted after thirty minutes to an hour of aerobic exercise, and fats become the more predominant energy source.

Nutrition and exercise

The ideal exercise and dietary program should use protein for muscle building and repair; carbohydrates should be used for sprinting, intense weightlifting, and other anaerobic exercise, as well as predominant fuel for routine activities; and fats should be used for prolonged aerobic activity. Fats are so abundant they cannot be depleted during prolonged, higher-intensity activities like brisk walking, jogging, or aerobic weightlifting.

You need carbohydrates in your diet to spare protein from being used as muscle fuel. If protein is broken down to be used as fuel for the exercising muscle instead of for repair and building, muscle growth will be inhibited. You also need carbohydrates since they are essential to the metabolic process that allows fats to be metabolized. To burn fats effectively, you need adequate carbohydrates in your diet.

To reach a goal of fat burning, muscle-and-strength building, and increased endurance, we need carbohydrates, protein, weight training, and aerobic exercise.

Exercise training has a major impact on protein metabolism, but this varies according to the type, duration, and intensity of the workout, and often the training status of the individual. There is a huge variation in sporting and exercise pursuits, ranging from brief explosive activities like sprinting or weightlifting to long, low-intensity activities like marathon running.

Where protein usage is concerned, the immediate response to exercise—protein breakdown, followed by increased rates of protein synthesis—is similar across the whole spectrum of activities. The immediate response after exercise is to replenish glycogen stores and repair muscle tissue. The intensity of training plays a key role in determining levels of tissue growth. Naturally, this intensity needs to be sufficient to challenge (overload) the body's systems. But there is a desirable middle ground between exercise which is not intense enough to cause overload and exercise which is so intense that it inhibits the metabolic responses responsible for synthesizing new body tissues.

Increased rates of protein synthesis may be maintained for up to 48 hours after exercise. Thus, the timing of recovery periods is crucial for stimulating optimum muscle-and-strength development. Inadequate recovery between exercise sessions can lead to overtraining and actually inhibit muscle growth.

In summary, the protein in a meal only becomes available for use by the body after it has been broken down into its constituent amino acids. The quality of any dietary protein is determined by its amino acids—and particularly by the presence of the eight amino acids which are not synthesized by the body and are, therefore, called "the essential amino acids." Egg white and whey protein approach the ideal protein source, since they have all the essential amino acids. Once digested, amino acids enter the body's amino acid pool and are distributed around the body according to requirements. Excess protein is converted to carbohydrates or stored as fat.

Physical activity in the form of resistance (weight) training (and to a lesser extent endurance exercise) increases the rate of both protein breakdown and synthesis. When combined with appropriately timed nutrient intake in the form of food or supplements, physical exercise has a major impact on growth of muscle tissue. Providing that certain nutrients (carbohydrates) are included in the intake, net protein synthesis will occur, and with regular resistance or endurance training, an increase in muscle and other tissues will be the result.

When should you eat in relation to exercise?

Proper timing of protein and carbohydrate intake can enhance strength training and conditioning. The needs can vary widely, depending on intensity of the workout, body weight, and muscle-building goals. A reasonable approach for the average person hoping to maintain conditioning and muscle tone is given below.

Before exercise
About ten minutes before your workout, drink a high-quality protein shake (usually whey protein) containing about 10 to 15 grams of protein.

After exercise
For fat loss, consume a protein shake with about 10 to 15 grams of protein.

For muscle building, consume a 10-to-15 gram protein shake that also contains about 15 to 20 grams of carbohydrates. The carbohydrates facilitate the uptake of protein and spare the breakdown of muscle protein.

Aerobic Exercise

Choose any aerobic exercise that works for you. It can be the simplest walking program, the *10,000-steps* program, jogging, treadmill, brisk walking, or running on a treadmill. You can do simple ten-, twenty- or thirty-minute programs, or for maximum results get involved with advanced aerobic and metabolic testing.

Aerobic exercise means "exercising with oxygen." You do exercise at an intensity that is low enough that adequate oxygen can be supplied to the exercising muscles, yet the intensity is high enough to increase both breathing rate and heart rate so there is an increase in oxygen uptake by the lungs and subsequent increased delivery of oxygen to the muscles. Brisk walking and jogging are typical examples.

Anaerobic means "without oxygen," which means the intensity of exercise is so high that not enough oxygen can be delivered to the exercising muscle to meet its needs. The exercise can only be sustained for very short periods (about thirty seconds) before there is a painful buildup of lactic acid in the muscles and the muscles fail to continue to contract. Sprinting and heavy weightlifting are examples of anaerobic exercise. Carbohydrates are the fuel used during anaerobic exercise. Carbohydrates are metabolized by several different mechanisms; some require oxygen and some do not. Fats cannot be used during anaerobic exercise, since to be used as a fuel fats require the presence of adequate oxygen.

How do you know you are doing aerobic exercise?

There are three ways to determine if you are exercising aerobically:

The talk test

As a rule of thumb, you can use the *"talk test"* to determine if you are exercising aerobically. If you exercise at an intensity where you feel slightly breathless but can still carry on a conversation without hesitating between words, then you have passed the *"talk test"* and are in your aerobic range. Though this heart-rate range can vary widely, the talk test is a useful guide to follow.

The target heart method

You can also use the well-known formula of 220 minus your age to determine your maximum heart rate, and then determine your target heart for fat burning to be 70 to 85% of your maximum heart rate. This will allow you will burn about 60% of your calories as fat. If you exercise, for instance, at 50% of your maximum heart rate, then 85 to 90% of your calories will be from fat, but you will have to exercise longer to burn the same total number of calories since you will be exercising less intensely and burning fewer calories per hour.

Advanced respiratory measurements

These methods are described in more detail in the following section. In brief, by measuring the amount of oxygen you inhale and the amount of carbon dioxide you exhale during exercise, the precise heart rate at which you burn more fats than carbohydrates can be determined. This is determined by the Respiratory Quotient discussed in more detail below.

What types of exercise are best for aerobic exercise?

In general, walking and jogging on a treadmill or outdoors are the simplest and best methods for aerobic exercise. Any exercise where you are bearing most of your weight will cause you to burn more calories per minute. So, walking will burn more calories than bicycling since on a bike part of your weight is being supported. Likewise, swimming, though a superb exercise, will usually burn fewer calories because of the water supporting the body. Stair-stepping machines are all excellent type of exercise. Each type of machine—bicycle, treadmill, or stair-stepping machine—tends to work slightly different muscle groups. So, if possible, it would be good to alternate the exercise on different days.

Physical conditioning is specific for the muscle groups that have been trained. For instance, you may be very consistent and capable on a treadmill, but find that you get winded climbing two flights of stairs. This usually has nothing to do with the function of your heart, but rather the muscles for stair climbing are not as conditioned as the muscles you trained while walking on the treadmill. The solution is to do more stair climbing. It's as simple as that.

Weight training is crucial to a successful exercise program. Weight training can also be aerobic if the weight you choose is light enough so that you can do about 15 repetitions and you do not need to strain or hold your breath to do the last contraction. Aerobic weight training will give you all the benefits to your heart without bulking up your muscles. As discussed later, weight training will allow you to burn up more fat calories throughout the day when you are using your arms during daily activities like deskwork. Adequate carbohydrate intake (as mentioned in the dietary section) will spare protein breakdown and help maintain muscle mass and strength.

Some basic guidelines for aerobic exercise

•   For weight loss, about 40 to 60 minutes five or more days per week of aerobic exercise are needed.

•   To decrease your cardiac risk, any exercise will do, but the most efficient way to get the greatest reduction of risk for the least amount of time would be to perform 30 to 40 minutes of aerobic exercise three to four times per week.

•   The 10,000-step method described below is the simplest method for weight loss and risk reduction since it is so simple to do, and yet you have some objective measurement of your exercise (that is, how many steps you do each day).

•   Split sessions are probably as effective as a continuous session—that is, three 10-minute sessions are as good as one 30-minute session. One study showed that three 10-minute sessions cause greater drops in triglyceride levels than one 30-minute session. So you can feel assured that split sessions are as reasonably effective as continuous sessions. If split sessions better fit your lifestyle, then do your exercise in split sessions.

Your exercise needs

In general, if you haven't been exercising, try to work up to 30 minutes, four to six times a week. Your doctor may make a different recommendation based on your health. If you can't carry on a conversation while you exercise, you may be overdoing it. It is best to alternate exercise days with rest days to prevent injuries.

All ages need exercise

Exercise is no less important for those in their sixties and seventies than it is for people half that age. No matter what your age, the benefits of exercise are the same—increased energy and self-esteem, conditioned heart and lungs, improved muscle tone, and greater function of bones and joints. The effects of certain chronic diseases—diabetes, high blood pressure, arthritis, and osteoporosis—can also be reduced by engaging in regular exercise.

There are many sports and activities you can choose from in order to achieve your fitness goals. The best choices, however, will be those activities that you truly enjoy. It's much easier to stay with something that's fun to do. Even walking for 30 minutes four to five days a week will go a long way in keeping you fit!

If you experience shortness of breath, dizziness, cold or clammy skin, nausea, or chest pains while exercising, stop exercising immediately and contact your physician.

Getting in Shape

Aerobic exercise

The Minimalist Approach—
10,000 steps per day

Many individuals cannot or will not undertake a vigorous program of structured or "health club" exercise. For them a minimalist approach may provide the necessary incentive to engage in additional activity. Minimalist exercise requires only a pedometer and two feet. The 10,000-step program originated in Japan in the mid 1960s after researchers noticed that women and men who walked 10,000 steps a day were healthier than those who exercised less. Subsequent studies from the University of Tennessee noticed that women aged 40 to 60 who walked 10,000 steps per day had significantly less body fat and narrower waists and hips.

Most people will walk 6,000 steps per day in their daily activities of sedentary work, childcare, and household activities. This is about three miles per day. Wear a pedometer for several days and calculate the average number of steps taken daily. Then simply add a brisk walk one, two, or three times daily to reach about 10,000 steps. This added activity takes about half an hour. Most sedentary people will lose several pounds and lower their blood pressure after a few weeks of 10,000 steps a day. It requires only an inexpensive pedometer and your desire to improve. The activity can be done anywhere.

There are lots of ways to raise your heart rate and reach 10,000 steps during your regular day. Take the stairs instead of the elevator. Walk during a coffee break or lunch. Walk to work or park at the end of the parking lot so you have to walk farther. Walk more briskly. Do housework at a quicker pace and more often (for example, vacuuming every day). Rake leaves, push the lawn mower, or do other yard work.

Walking or jogging
(outdoors or on a treadmill)

Walking is a great way to achieve overall fitness year-round. It strengthens your cardiovascular system, tones and limbers up your muscles, and burns off unwanted calories. Walking at a brisk pace gives you the same aerobic benefits as jogging!

Walking also reduces blood pressure, improves sleeping habits, helps digestion, alleviates constipation, raises metabolism, and helps to reduce loss of bone mass in post-menopausal women.

If you are thinking about joining the more than 10 million Americans now jogging, be sure your jogging equipment—your cardiopulmonary respiratory system, feet, and legs—is in good working order!

Stretch before and after exercise

- **Upper body twist** – Stand with your hands on your hips. Slowly turn your upper body as far as possible to the left for a count of 5. Turn to the right and hold for a count of 5. Repeat ten times.

- **Upper body stretch** – Stand with your back straight and arms to your sides. Stretch arms straight out in front of you and hold for a count of 5. Return arms to sides. Repeat ten times. Now, stretch arms straight in back of you until shoulder blades touch. Hold for a count of 5. Return arms to sides. Repeat ten times.

- **Hamstring stretch** – Place the heel of your right foot up on a bench. Straighten out your right leg and keep your left knee (the leg you're standing on) slightly bent. Reach for the toes of your right foot with both hands. Hold the stretch for 15 to 20 seconds, and then repeat with other leg. Do this several times, gently at first. Stretch slowly and steadily—don't bounce!

  Start exercising a few weeks in advance—about the same time of day you'll be playing golf or tennis. Walk 20 to 30 minutes a day, three to four times a week.

Fitness in minutes

We've all had days when we think there's not enough time to squeeze in a decent workout, so we decide to forgo it altogether. But where fitness is concerned, something is better than nothing. Don't get caught in the trap of thinking that if you don't have the time to do a complete workout, you shouldn't even bother.

You may not be able to do the recommended 20 to 30 minutes of cardiovascular work, but short, efficient workouts that combine strength training and aerobics can help raise energy levels, tone the body, and relieve stress. You don't even need any gym equipment or videos. Just think back to those calisthenics most of us used to do in school gym class—a few push-ups, some jumping jacks, and a few crunches. The key is to keep moving and maximize every move.

On the following pages are workout plans for 10, 20, and 30 minutes, which you can do just about anywhere, anytime. Mix and match the exercises for variety, but don't forget to warm up, cool down, and stretch. And remember, activity of any kind is better than nothing. If you don't want to do a set workout, find something you like to do and do it. If all you feel like doing is going on a brisk walk or dancing for 20 minutes, that's fine too. It's all about getting you moving. Try to enjoy yourself while you're at it.

10-Minute Workout

- *1 minute – Warm-up.* March in place or walk around.
- *2 minutes – Lunges.* Step back with one leg and drop that knee to the floor allowing the front knee to bend. Divide into sets of 10 to 20 per leg. Make sure that you don't extend the knee of your forward foot beyond your toes.
- *1 minute – Squats (deep knee bends).* Keeping the knee directly over the foot, drop your bottom until thighs are parallel to the floor, then stand up. Never drop below a 90-degree angle at the knee.
  - *2 minutes – Regular Push-ups. With either knee touching the floor or straight behind, military style, lower the chest to the floor and back up. Perform as many as you can in a two-minute period, even if you have to take a break a number to times.*
- *2 minutes – Abdominal Crunches.* Lie flat on your back with your feet drawn up to your bottom. Put your hands behind your head. Support your head and look straight up at the ceiling while crunching your abdominals and lifting your shoulders off the ground.
- *2 minutes – Stretch.* Put your feet out in front of you while you are sitting on the floor. Take both hands and, without bending your knees, reach for your toes. You are fairly flexible when you can grab your feet while your knees are straight and hold for 30 seconds. Lie down on your stomach and lift your upper body off the ground while your pelvis remains in contact with the floor. Hold for 30 seconds.

20-Minute Workout

- *2 minutes – Warm-up.* March in place or walk around.
- *2 minutes – Cardiovascular.* Jog in place or jump rope to get your heart rate up.
- *2 minutes – Squats (deep knee bends).* Keeping the knee directly over the foot, drop your bottom until thighs are parallel to the floor, then stand up. Never drop below a 90-degree angle at the knee.
- *2 minutes – Calf Raises.* Place the ball of the foot on a step with the heel dropping below. Rise up onto your toes and slowly drop. Alternate legs. If you don't have a step, the floor will work.
- *2 minutes – Cardiovascular.* Do some jumping jacks or run in place to get your heart pumping again.
- *2 minutes – Lunges.* Step back with one leg and drop that knee to the floor, allowing the front knee to bend. Divide into sets of 10 to 20 per leg. Make certain that you don't extend the knee of your forward foot beyond your toes.
- *1 minute – Triceps Dips.* With your hands slightly behind you, grip the edge of a desk, table, chair, or other sturdy surface. Using your legs for support, lower your body and then push back up.
- *2 minutes – Regular Push-ups.* With your legs extended straight behind you or knees on the floor and arms spread at shoulder width, lower your chest to the floor and push back up. Do as many as you can in two minutes, no matter how many breaks you have to take.
- *1 minute – Bicycle Crunches.* With hands clasped behind the head, bring the right elbow to the left knee and alternate, bringing the left elbow to the right knee.
- *1 minute – Cool Down.* March in place or walk around.
- *3 minutes – Stretch.* Do a number of various stretches and hold each one for 30 seconds.

30-Minute Workout

- *2 minutes – Warm-up.* March in place or walk around.
- *2 minutes – Squats.* Keeping the knee directly over the foot, drop your bottom until your thighs are parallel to the floor, then stand up. Never drop below a 90-degree angle at the knee.
- *3 minutes – Cardiovascular.* Jog in place to get your heart rate up.
- *2 minutes – Lunges.* Step back with one leg and drop that knee to the floor, allowing the front knee to bend. Divide into sets of 10 to 20 on each leg. Never drop below a 90-degree angle at the knee.
- *2 minutes – Cardiovascular.* Do some jumping jacks or jog in place or jump rope to get your heart going.
- *2 minutes – Calf Raises.* Place the ball of the foot on a step with the heel dropping below. Rise up onto your toes and slowly drop. Alternate legs. If you don't have a step, the floor will work.
- *2 minutes – Cardiovascular.* Jog in place.
- *3 minutes – Leg Lifts.* With hands and knees on the floor, bring one knee in toward your chest, and then extend it straight behind you. Alternate legs. Try to keep your leg straight as you lift.
- *2 minutes – Narrow Push-ups.* Place hands on the floor with thumbs touching. Lower your chest to the floor and push back up. Don't allow your buttocks to stick up in the air while doing this exercise.
- *3 minutes – Triceps Dips.* With your hands slightly behind you, grip the edge of a desk, chair, or other stable surface. Using your legs for support, lower your body and then push back up. Do as many as you can for three minutes, even if you have to take a number of breaks.
- *2 minutes – Regular Push-ups.* With your legs extended straight behind you or knees on the floor and arms spread at shoulder width, lower your chest to the floor and push

back up. Do as many as you can in two minutes, no matter how many breaks you have to take.

- *1 minute – Cool Down.* March in place or walk around.
- *4 minutes – Stretch.* Do a number of various stretches and hold each one for 30 seconds.

Consistency counts

The body is wonderful. It treats you right if you do the same to it. Let's give an example: The more consistent you are, the more trained your muscles become in getting rid of fat (fat metabolism). Trained muscles burn fat more efficiently, even during rest when you aren't doing a thing. Some studies suggest that the body burns extra fat for up to 24 hours after a good exercise session. That, plus your personalized weight-management and nutrition plan, means that you will burn more fat more consistently, even when you are sleeping. *The OC Diet 50/25/25* nutrition plan actually creates a more efficient system. You have more energy, sleep better, maintain safe levels of cholesterol and blood pressure— even handle stress like a pro. In other words, you are a completely better you!

Fluid intake

Our bodies are about 70% water. They can't function without it. Drink water throughout you exercise regimen, at least 8 ounces every 30 minutes. Weigh yourself before and after exercise. If your weight is down after exercise, drink that amount in water. Interestingly enough, most people only drink water after they "feel" thirsty. The problem with that is by the time you are thirsty, your body is already beginning to dehydrate. Drinking enough purified or filtered water throughout the day—one half of your body weight in ounces—is the perfect way to cleanse your body of unwanted toxins. Drink enough water each day, along with staying on your personalized nutrition and exercise plan, and you will actually lose weight attributed to excess water retention.

Advanced Aerobic Testing

Advanced aerobic testing uses newly devised monitors to more precisely determine the parameters of metabolism. These types of tests are measured in certain physical fitness centers under the guidance of exercise physiologists.

Methods of testing

A mask is used to measure the amount of oxygen you consume (called VO_2) and to measure the amount of carbon dioxide you exhale (called VCO_2). A ratio is calculated called the *Respiratory Quotient (RQ)*, which is the ratio of carbon dioxide (CO_2) output and the quantity of oxygen (O_2) inhaled. The data is continually fed into a computer, along with heart rate, body mass index, and other parameters. A continuous graph of the measurements is created and recorded during the testing period.

When this is measured at rest after a twelve-hour fast, it will determine your *Resting Metabolic Rate.* This ratio can also be measured during exercise. When the *RQ* is measured during exercise, it can be used to determine your target heart rate for aerobic exercise. This proportion of oxygen consumption and carbon dioxide production is measured throughout the testing period while you exercise on a stationary bicycle or treadmill until you reach a certain heart rate (85% of the maximum for you age). This is called *submaximal fitness testing,* or you are exercised to the point of exhaustion, it is called *maximal fitness testing.* Either method will determine at what heart rate you start to burn up more carbohydrates than fats before you enter your anaerobic threshold heart rate.

Remember, we are trying to scientifically determine a heart rate at which maximal fat burning occurs. Different fuels have different *RQ* numbers: fat = 0.70, protein = 0.82, and carbohydrates = 1.00. At rest in a fasting state the usual *RQ* = 0.82. At any heart rate you burn various ratios of carbohydrates and fats (since protein is rarely used as fuel unless starving conditions occur or severe carbohydrate restriction).

Three metabolic measurements can be determined and used to maximize your weight loss and conditioning to improve your overall cardiovascular health

1. Your *resting metabolic rate*
    This tells you how many calories you use at rest just for bodily functions like breathing, digestion, pumping blood, and maintaining body temperature to maintain life. This accounts for about 60 to 70% of the calories we use up each day. Then, based on your level of activity, the total number of calories you can consume for weight loss or weight maintenance can be determined.

2. Your *target heart rate* for aerobic exercise
    A heart rate that causes your *RQ* to approach 0.70 means you are in the maximum fat-burning zone, and if the *RQ* approaches 1.0, you are in the maximum carbohydrate zone. These numbers are continuously recorded on a computer screen during testing, and the heart rate where fat burning starts to increase is plotted. You then use this heart rate for your maximum fat-burning-exercise target heart rate. In four to eight weeks, you body conditioning may change and another fitness test will be needed. This will be the most scientific method of achieving weight loss when combined with *The OC Diet 50/25/25* meal plans.

For improved physical conditioning for sports training and to improve your cardiorespiratory fitness, you would want a heart rate toward the higher numbers of the aerobic heart-rate zone, compared to a heart rate toward the lower range for maximum fat burning. Note that for either, maximum fat burning or maximum physical conditioning, the target heart rates will still be in an aerobic range.

How does this compare to other methods of determining target heart rates? We mentioned two basic and simple methods to determine your target heart rate for maximum fat burning:

a. The *"talk test,"* which assumes that as your respiratory rate increases, the uptake of oxygen increases, so you are therefore doing aerobic exercise. With practice many people can correlate their perceived sense of breathlessness with a certain heart rate. The "talk test" further assumes that when you are breathing so hard that it is difficult to carry on a conversation without hesitating between sentences, you are now beyond the capacity of your system to provide adequate oxygen to your muscles. So, you are now entering your anaerobic threshold. We don't want to enter the anaerobic threshold for long, because we tend to burn more carbohydrates than fats, so we want to maintain our exercise in the aerobic level of intensity.

b. The *target-heart-rate zone* (based on the 220 minus your age formula) is also based on assumptions that most people will be in the aerobic fat-burning range if they follow the formula and exercise to keep their heart rate in that zone for the 30 to 40 minutes of exercise.

The benefits of these two approaches are obvious: they are extremely simple to follow, and at most you may need a simple heart-rate monitor (of which there are numerous and varied types). The drawback of the "talk test" and the target-heart-rate formula is that they can be inaccurate, since heart-rate ranges can vary tremendously. There is very likely a heart rate for you to exercise at that can be 10 to 20 beats higher or lower than either method determined for you, and which will still get you to maximal fat burning. Which method you use depends on a number of things— access to advanced testing, money, time, and commitment. For sure, any of these methods will work fairly well if you just do the exercise faithfully. The advanced method may produce weight-lose gains more quickly.

3. Your *level of physical fitness* to determine your cardio-vascular conditioning.

How is physical fitness measured? The maximal amount of oxygen you consume at peak exercise is the most reliable way of measuring your level of cardio respiratory fitness. This maximal oxygen uptake is called the *VO$_2$ max. (volume of oxygen maximal),* which is reported in milliliters of O$_2$ per kilogram of body weight per minute. This number is measured at the time the RQ is determined, but it can also be measured independently on less sophisticated monitors.

Strength-training Exercises

How to begin

Strength training (also referred to as weight training or resistance exercises) can be done at home or at a fitness center. We strongly suggest that you opt for a professionally supervised program of strength training. This is because, for best results, your program should include overload and progressive-resistance portions, all performed in a specific order. This will dictate the results that you see.

Below are some tips to maximize your weight-training efforts that, when combined with any of the aerobic exercise mentioned above and **The OC Heart Diet** nutritional plan, will give you the greatest opportunity to maintain your heart health.

Why strength training works
- It increases lean muscle mass
- It increases metabolism
- It increases fat burning

The rationale of strength training

It's best to find a professional trainer or health club in order to receive the exact training method that is right for you. It will not "pump you up," but it will create a new and better you, one that can enjoy life to the limit. By the way, women will not become bulky on a regular strength-training routine, simply because they have inadequate levels of testosterone for building large muscle mass.

Strength training is an essential part of present-day exercise programs. Strength training isn't only for athletes or those who want sculptured bodies and bulging muscles. Everyone of any age —especially women—will benefit from strength training. Muscles that are in tone are very efficient burners of fat. An arm that is toned and muscular will burn more fat and calories throughout the day while doing daily chores than an arm that is flabby and not muscular. Anyone—regardless of age—has the ability to improve muscle mass and strength, though as we age it becomes more difficult to build large bulging muscles as seen in younger people doing similar exercise. Part of the explanation is probably due to dropping testosterone levels in men and women. (Women have testosterone also, though much lower than in a similarly aged man and much lower than their estrogen levels.)

Strong muscles have the ability to protect our joints, reduce osteoporosis (especially in women), and improve our cholesterol levels. In addition, muscles that are toned and strong are more efficient users of oxygen. They ease the workload on the heart by being able to perform a task more efficiently. A toned muscle can extract more oxygen from the same amount of blood than can a deconditioned muscle; therefore, the heart can pump less vigorously for the muscle to do the same amount of work. This is especially true in heart patients that have reduced function of the pumping action of their hearts. Since the output of the heart is reduced, toned and strong muscles are more efficient in easing the burden on the impaired heart.

Before embarking on any exercise program, you should get approval from your doctor if you have been very sedentary and are middle aged or older!

Weight-training Basics

There are different types of strength-training applications, namely isometric and isotonic training. Isometric means you apply force by contracting your muscle, but you do not shorten the muscle. An example would be if you try to lift the end of a table that is bolted to the floor. You contract your bicep to lift the table edge, but the bicep muscle does not shorten because you cannot move the table. Isometric exercises are not very effective compared to isotonic exercise.

The best all-around type of strength training you can follow is the isotonic technique. This involves the concentric contraction (shortening) of the muscle and subsequent eccentric contraction (lengthening) of the muscle while the muscle is under stress (weight bearing). This is the familiar weightlifting motion where the weight is lifted as the muscle contracts (for example, the typical bicep curl). The concentric portion (contracting muscle movement) of the exercise is the portion that most people concentrate on. However, the eccentric portion (lengthening the muscle as you release the weight) is as important, and some studies show it is the more important portion of the exercise.

For instance, if you have a weight and do a bicep curl, the curling up and contacting the muscle (the concentric movement) should be steady and deliberate. However, when you relax the arm to lower the weight, it is important to lower the weight slowly and deliberately (the eccentric movement) so there is tension on the muscle rather than suddenly releasing the arm.

Guidelines to Maximize the Benefits of Weight Training

What exercises to do?
Exercises that use multiple body parts are called compound exercises. Compound exercises burn up more calories and speed muscle development. Bench presses and pushups not only involve the chest muscles, but the back and arms as well. Squatting exercises, rowing, lunges, overhead presses (like military presses), pull-ups, and chin-ups are some of the exercises that should be incorporated into the body-specific exercises like arm and leg curls. If you do specific body-part exercises the same day as compound exercises, do the compound exercises first.

How much weight and how many repetitions to use?
The amount of weight and number of repetitions you use depends on what you want to accomplish. It is important that you vary the repetitions and weight every four weeks.
- For fat-burning and toning exercises, lighter weights and more repetitions are required. This becomes "aerobic weightlifting"; that is, you choose a weight light enough that you can do 12 to 15 repetitions to complete one set, such that the last repetition is easy enough that you can do it without holding your breath.
- For muscle building, you should choose a weight that you can do 4 to 8 repetitions to complete one set with a weight heavy enough that the last repetition is somewhat difficult, but you can still maintain proper form.

How many sets of exercise? How much rest between sets?
A set means the completion of a group of repetitions. If you do arm curls and lift the weight eight times in a row, that is one set of eight repetitions. To exercise any muscle group, you may want to do two or three sets of 4 to 15 repetitions per set, depending on what you want to accomplish. For example:

- For fat burning, you need about 15 to 25 sets per workout session. So you might work six different muscle groups. You would have six different exercises with three sets per exercise. There will be less resting between sets and more calories burned. Rest 30 to 60 seconds between sets.
- Strength and muscle building require about 12 to 15 sets per workout session. So you might work six different muscle groups. You would have six different exercises with two sets per exercise. However, more weight is lifted but with fewer repetitions and more rest between sets. Rest two to three minutes between sets.

How often should you do weight training?
- For fat burning, do three total body workouts per week. Total body workouts mean you are exercising the upper and lower body the same day. You should have at least one day of rest in between.
- For strength and muscle building, alternate upper body one day and lower body the next day. So four workout sessions per week with three days of rest.

When should you eat in relation to exercise?

Before exercise
About ten minutes before your work out, drink a high-quality protein shake (usually whey protein) of about 10 to 15 grams of protein.

After exercise
For fat loss, consume a protein shake with about 10 to 15 grams of protein.

For muscle building, consume a 10-to-15-gram protein shake that also contains about 15 to 20 grams of carbohydrates. The carbohydrates facilitate the uptake of protein and spare the breakdown of muscle protein.

How long should you weight train?

Depending on your goals, 30 to 40 minutes three times per week should be sufficient for muscle toning and conditioning.

How can you prevent injury and muscle soreness?

Micro tears in the muscle cause muscle soreness after exercise. The soreness usually improves with exercise on subsequent days. If there is residual muscle soreness, doing the same exercise at half the intensity on subsequent days will help the soreness. However, if there is severe pain with exercise, numbness, or weakness, the exercise should be stopped until you are seen by a physician.

Should you do weight training or aerobic exercise first?

- For fat loss, there is probably little difference if aerobic or weight training is done first.
- For muscle building, weight training before aerobic exercise will provide better strength and muscle-building gains.

Fitness Summary

Exercise of any type will benefit you. Choose the type that fits your lifestyle and experiment with the various programs discussed above. You will eventually settle into a program that is enjoyable and sustainable.

1. Do your exercises at least four days per week and up to seven days per week for maximum weight loss.
2. Add weight training two to three times per week.
3. Stretch.
4. Be consistent.
5. Be patient.
6. Adhere to *The OC Heart Diet 50/25/25* nutritional program.

TO YOUR SUCCESS!!

Part IV

Glossary of Heart Terms

Addendum A

Addendum B

Addendum C

Addendum D

Afterword

Glossary of Heart Terms

Ablation
A *procedure* used to correct certain types of heart rhythm disorders.

ACE inhibitors:
A group of medications that help relax blood vessels. They are used to treat high blood pressure and heart failure. For people with heart failure, ACE inhibitors have been shown to prolong life and minimize symptoms.

Acute myocardial infarction:
The formation of a localized area of ischemic necrosis produced by occlusion of the arterial supply or the venous drainage of the part occurring during the period when circulation to a region of the heart is obstructed and necrosis is occurring

Amino acid: An organic compound that's a basic part of a protein.

Aerobic exercise
Repetitive, rhythmic exercise involving the body's large muscle group**s**. *Examples* include brisk walking, cycling and swimming.

Aneurysm
A balloon-like swelling of the artery.

Angina
Heaviness or tightness in the centre of the chest which may typically spread to the arms, neck and jaw. Caused when the arteries become so narrow that not enough oxygen-containing blood can reach the heart muscle when its demands are high - such as during exercise.

Angiogram
An *X-ray picture* of the blood vessels outlined by injected contrast material which shows where the arteries are narrowed and how narrow they have become.

Angioplasty
A *treatment* to improve the blood supply through an artery by expanding (dilating) a narrowed segment.

Anti-platelet drug
A *drug* to prevent the clotting of blood by reducing platelet stickiness.

Anticoagulant
A drug used to reduce the risk of blood clots forming. Clots consist of two elements - platelets (small blood cells) clumped together, and a protein called fibrin. Anticoagulants act by helping to prevent fibrin from forming.

Antioxidants
Vitamins and other substances found mainly in vegetables and fruit.

Aorta
The main *artery l*eading out of the left side of the heart which gives off various branches to supply the whole body with blood.

Arrhythmia
A disorder of the *heart rhythm.*

Artery
A blood vessel carrying oxygenated blood from the heart to the rest of the body.

Aspirin
An anti-platelet *drug* used to help prevent blood clots forming.

Atheroma
Fatty material that can build up within the walls of the arteries. When atheroma affects the coronary arteries, it can cause angina, heart attack or sudden death. When it affects the arteries to the brain, it may cause a stroke. When it affects the leg arteries, it causes peripheral arterial disease. Atheroma can build up silently for many years before it causes trouble.

Atherosclerosis
The build-up of *fatty materials* within the walls of the arteries.

Atria
The two upper chambers of the *heart.* They act as collecting chambers to fill the ventricles (the two lower pumping chambers of the heart).

Atrial fibrillation
A type of *arrhythmia (*irregular heartbeat) in which the atria (the upper two chambers of the heart) beat very rapidly, at up to 400 beats per minute and the ventricles respond by beating quickly and irregularly. Atrial fibrillation can produce quite unpleasant palpitations and

sometimes breathlessness, and in some cases the fast irregular rhythm may lead to a clot forming in the heart.

Atrio-ventricular node
The part of the heart through which the *electrical impulses* pass from the atria to the ventricles, to stimulate ventricular contraction and heart pump function.

Blood pressure
The *pressure* in the main arterial system which is usually measured indirectly in the arm.

Body mass index (BMI) A formula to work out whether a person is overweight, calculated by dividing weight (in kilograms) by height (in metres²).

Bradycardia
A slow heart rate.

Calcium channel blocker (calcium antagonist)
A drug that is used for angina and high blood pressure.

Cardiac
To do with the heart.

Cardiac arrest
When the *heart stops pumping*, due to no electrical activity or disorganized ineffective electrical activity.

Cardiac enzyme tests
Blood tests to measure the level of certain enzymes in the blood released by heart muscle during a heart attack

Cardiologist
Doctor specializing in heart disease.

Cardiomyopathy
A **disease** of the heart muscle.

Cardiovascular
To do with the heart and blood vessels.

Catheter ablation therapy
A *procedure* used to correct certain types of heart rhythm disorders.

Cholesterol
A fatty substance mainly made in the body by the liver. *Cholesterol* plays a vital role in the functioning of every cell wall throughout the body. It is also the material which the body uses to make other vital chemicals. However, too much cholesterol in the blood can increase the risk of getting coronary heart disease.

Cholesterol-lowering drug
A drug to lower the blood cholesterol level.

Clot-buster
A drug used when there is an urgent need to dissolve a clot - for example during a heart attack.

Congenital heart disease
Heart *disease* caused by abnormalities of the heart or major blood vessels which are due to abnormal development of the fetus and which are present at birth.

Congenital:
Present at and existing from the time of birth.

Contrast Echocardiogram:
That in which the ultrasonic beam detects tiny bubbles produced by intravascular injection of a liquid of a small amount of carbon dioxide gas.

Coronary artery bypass grafting (CABG):
A surgical procedure in which a segment of vein or artery is used to restore blood flow to a diseased artery supplying blood to the heart.

Coronary artery disease:
A progressive disease in which blockages develop in the blood vessels supplying blood to the heart muscle. The blockages can be caused by elevated blood cholesterol, smoking, diabetes or high blood pressure, among other factors. If the blockages become severe, a heart attack can occur, leading to damage of the heart muscle.

Coronary ischemia:
Localized areas of heart tissue that receive insufficient oxygen supply due to reduced blood. This is caused by narrowed/blocked coro-

nary arteries and sometimes results in angina pectoris or myocardial infarction.

Coronary arteries
The *arteries* that arise from the beginning of the aorta and supply blood to the heart muscle.

Coronary thrombosis
When a *blood clot* forms in a narrowed coronary artery and causes a *heart attack*.

Defibrillation
A emergency *procedure* to correct ventricular fibrillation and restore a regular heart rhythm by delivering an electric shock through the chest wall to the heart.

Diabetes
A *disease* caused by a lack of insulin or an increased resistance of the body to insulin - a risk factor for cardiovascular disease.

Diastolic blood pressure
When measuring *blood pressure,* the diastolic blood pressure is the lowest.

Edema
Swelling.

Echocardiogram
An *ultrasound* picture of the heart which shows the structure of the heart and pump function.

Electrocardiogram
Also known as *'ECG'*. A test to record the rhythm and electrical activity of the heart.

Electrophysiological testing
A procedure used to detect and give information about abnormal heart rhythms.

Enzymes
Proteins that help stimulate chemical actions in the body.

Endothelial: the layer of epithelial cells that lines the cavities of the heart, the serous cavities, and the lumina of the blood and lymph vessels.

Endothelium: I
Lning of blood vessels.

Exercise electrocardiogram
When the rhythm and the *electrical activity* of the heart is recorded while the person is exercising, usually on a treadmill. This may show evidence of ischaemia or insufficient coronary artery blood flow with the increased demand of exercise.

Familial hypercholesterolaemia
An inherited condition in which the blood *cholesterol* level is very high.

Fibrate
A drug used to reduce cholesterol and triglyceride levels in the blood.

Fibrillation
When something quivers uncontrollably. See: *atrial fibrillation.*

Generic name
Official name (for example, of a drug).

Heart attack
When one of the coronary arteries becomes blocked by a blood clot and part of the heart is starved of oxygen leading to *muscle death.*

Heart block
When the *electrical impulse* traveling from the atria to the ventricles in the heart sometimes don't conduct properly.

Heart failure
When the pumping action of the *heart* is inadequate to meet the demands of the body.

Heart rate
The number of heart beats per minute.

High blood pressure
High pressure in the arterial circulation. This happens if the walls of the larger arteries lose their natural elasticity and become more rigid, and the smaller vessels become narrower. It can also result from an increase in the circulating blood volume. Also called *hypertension.*

High density lipoprotein
The protective cholesterol. Also referred to as *HDL cholesterol.*

Holter monitoring
Continuously recording an electrocardiogram (ECG) over 24 hours. The recorder produces an electrocardiogram which can be analyzed later.

Hypercholesterolaemia
When there is an excessive amount of *cholesterol* in the blood.
Hypertension
Associated with *high blood pressure.*

Implantable cardiovertor defibrillator
A *device* which is implanted within the chest wall. It monitors the heart's rhythm and senses disturbance in rhythm, and treats the rhythm as programmed by pacing, cardioversion or defibrillation.

Intermittent claudication
A cramp like pain mostly in the calf and leg muscles, brought on by walking and relieved by rest. Usually a symptom of *peripheral vascular disease* (PVD).

Ischaemia
Inadequate blood supply.

Ischaemic heart disease
Inadequate flow of blood through the *coronary arteries* to the heart. Also known as coronary heart disease.

Left ventricular hypertrophy
When the heart muscle of the left ventricle becomes abnormally thickened. Often associated with *hypertension.*

Lipid lowering drug
A drug used to lower *cholesterol* levels.

Lipids
Fatty substances in the blood including cholesterol and tryglycerides.

Lipoproteins
Combinations of lipids and proteins. *Cholesterol* has a special transport system for reaching all the cells which need it. It uses the blood circulation as its road network and is carried on vehicles made up of

proteins. This combination of cholesterol and proteins are called lipoproteins.

Mitral valve
The *valve* that regulates the flow of blood from the left atrium to the left ventricle.

Monounsaturated fat
A type of *fat* found in foods such as olive oil, walnut oil, grapeseed oil, avocado and in some margarines and spreads. Monounsaturated fats can help lower the blood level of LDL cholesterol, but do not lower the level of the protective HDL cholesterol level.

MRI:
One of the most powerful tools for viewing the internal organs; produces remarkably clear images of the heart, making it especially useful for detecting and assessing heart masses like lumps or tumors.

MUGA:
A method of labeling red blood cells to image the chambers of the heart and its function.

Myocardial infarction (MI):
The medical term for a heart attack.

Myocardium
The *heart muscle.*

Noninvasive:
Used to describe a procedure that doesn't penetrate the skin.

Occluded:
Obstructed or cut off.

Omega 3
A type of fatty acid found in fish oils. Eating foods containing omega three fatty acids can help prevent blood clotting and help reduce triglyceride levels.

Palpitations
An awareness of a *fast or irregular heartbeat.*

Paroxysmal
Intermittent.

Percutaneous:
Performed through the skin

Peripheral vascular disease
Disease of the blood vessels that supply the blood to the limbs, commonly known as *PVD.*

PET:
A refinement of SPECT technology, providing a clearer pictire of blood flow and heart function. These images can assist physicians in diagnosing coronary artery disease, hardening of the arteries, and blood flow, as well as assessing coronary bypass grafts and heart transplantation.

Platelets
Small blood cells that help to form a clot.

Plaque: A fatty substance made up of fat, cholesterol and mineral deposits that can develop on the inside of arterial walls.

Polyunsaturated fats
A type of *fat* found in foods from plant and fish such as cornflower oil, sunflower oil, fish oil and some margarines and spreads.

Pulmonary
To do with the lungs.

Pulmonary artery
The *artery* that carries blood from the heart to the lungs.

Pulmonary valve
The *valve* which regulates the flow of blood from the right ventricle to the pulmonary artery.

Reductase inhibitor: product that helps to limit the amount of cholesterol produced by the body, found in "statin" drugs.

Resuscitation
Actions to restore breathing and circulation.

Revascularisation
A procedure that either *opens up the existing blood vessels or bypasses the blockage* of the coronary arteries.

Risk factor for coronary heart disease
Something that can increase the risk of getting coronary heart disease. *Risk factors* include smoking, high blood pressure, raised cholesterol, physical inactivity, obesity, diabetes and a family history of heart disease.

Saturated fat
A type of *fat* found mainly in food from animal sources particularly diary and meat products.

Sinus bradycardia
A normal but slow *heart rhythm.*

SPECT:
Involves a series of cameras rapidly imaging the heart from different angles and dimensions to study blood flow to the heart

Statin
A drug used to control cholesterol levels.

Stenosis
Obstruction. Valve stenosis is when a *heart valve* does not open fully and obstructs the flow of blood.

Stent
A short tube of metal mesh inserted at the part of the artery which is to be widened by *coronary angioplasty.*

Systolic blood pressure
Is the top number of a *blood pressure,* which occurs when the heart is contracting to push the blood around the body.

Tachycardia
A *fast heart rate.*

Thrombolysis
Drug treatment to help dissolve a clot blocking an artery, during a *heart attack.*

Thrombosis
Formation of a blood *clot* in the blood vessels or heart that leads to a *heart attack.*

Thrombus
A blood *clot.*

Tissue valve
Valve from a animal or human, sometimes used to replace a damaged or *diseased heart valve.*

Thoracotomy:
Incision of the chest wall.

Transoesophageal echocardiography
Also called a TOE. A *procedure* that involves taking detailed pictures of the heart from the esphagus, which lies behind the heart.

Tricsupid valve
The *valve* that regulates the flow of blood from the right atrium to the right ventricle.

Triglycerides
A *fatty* substance found in the blood.

Unsaturated fat
A type of *fat* found mainly in foods from plants and fish sources. They include monounsaturated fats and polyunsaturated fats.

Unstable angina:
Angina pectoris that is marked by sudden changes in severity, length or the level of exertion required to trigger an attack.

Valve incompetence
When a *valve* does not close properly, allowing blood to leak back-wards.

Valve stenosis
Narrowing of a *valve.*

Valvular heart disease
When one of more of the four *heart valves* are diseased or damaged.

Vascular
To do with blood vessels.

Vasculopathy:
Any disorder of blood vessels

Vasospastic:
Spasm of the blood vessels, decreasing their caliber

Vein
The **vessel** carrying blood away from the various parts of the body to the heart.

Ventricles
The two main pumping *chambers of the heart.*

Ventricular fibrillation
A life threatening disturbance of the heart rhythm whereby the ventricles of the heart initiate impulses at a fast irregular rate causing the ventricles to fibrillate or quiver, which leads to insufficient blood to be pumped around the body.

Ventricular tachycardia
A *fast heart rate* where the electrical impulses are initiated by the ventricles of the heart

VLDL: Very low-density lipoprotein; the liver converts VLDL into LDL by removing triglyerides from it.

Xanthomas: Tiny cholesterol-filled bumps that may appear on the skin as a symptom of severe hypercholesterolemia

Addendum A
Heart Scan Centers

T he following is a list of EBCT heart–scan centers avail able as of this writing. Remember, new centers may be opening or changing phone numbers at any time. Some states do not have scanning centers at this time. Whenever you choose to have your heart scan done, it is important that the imaging center uses an *EBCT scanner.* Ask them specifically if they perform an *EBCT scan.* Don't be confused with the name "ultrafast", which was the name used early on for *EBCT* scanners. Nowadays, some conventional CT centers may refer to their new conventional multislice CT as ultrafast. If at all possible, seek out an EBCT scan center. Remember, *only EBCT scans have low radiation and high accuracy,* and they should be the only type of CT scan used for coronary calcium screening whenever available

The best centers will be associated with a cardiology group that will interpret the heart scans and make recommendations for treatment based on the latest cardiology research. If you have a choice of a center in your area, go to one that is associated with a cardiology group. Most centers also do full–body scans and virtual colonoscopy. If you want a full–body or virtual colonoscopy, you should schedule that at the time of your heart scan, since the time involved and radiation exposure will be less.

Alabama
Health & Longevity Center at the McCollough Institute
350 Cypress Bend Boulevard
Gulf Shores, AL 36547
Phone: 251–967–7000

Arkansas
Scan America
808 South Walton Boulevard
Bentonville, AR 72712
Phone: 479–254–0580

Arizona
Arizona Heart Institutes
Heart Test and Lung Test
2632 North 20th Street
Phoenix, AZ 85006
Phone: 602–212–100

Southwest Preventive Imaging
4511 N. Campbell Avenue, Suite 100
Tucson, AZ 85718
Phone: 520–529–4013

BodyScan Imaging Center Scottsdale
909 N. Scottsdale Road
Tempe, AZ 85281
Phone: 866–306–2639

California (northern)
Heartscan – San Francisco
389 Oyster Point Boulevard
South San Francisco, CA 94080
Phone: 650–872–7800

HeartScan – Walnut Creek
2161 Ygnacio Valley Road
Walnut Creek, CA 94598
Phone: 925–939–3003

California Heart Scan
2288 Auburn Boulevard, Suite 102
Sacramento, CA 95677
Phone: 916–923–9900

California (southern)
Los Angeles:
Tower Imaging HeartCheck
465 N. Roxbury Drive, Suite 103
Beverly Hills, CA 90210
Phone: 1–800–NEW–TEST

Cedars – Sinai Medical Center
8700 Beverly Boulevard, Suite 1240
Los Angeles, CA 90048
Phone: 310–423–8000

Harbor – UCLA Medical Center
St. Johns Cardiovascular Building, RB-2
1124 West Carson Street
Torrance, CA 90502–3631
Phone: 310–222–2773

UCLA Medical Center
Department of Thoracic Radiology
10833 Le Conte Avenue
Los Angeles, CA 90024
Phone: 310–794–9729

Orange County:
OC Vital Imaging
1120 W. La Veta, Suite 150
Orange, CA 92868
Phone: 714–558–2040
(Associated with the authors of
The OC Heart Diet and the cardiologists
of the Orange County Heart Institute)
www.ocvitalimaging.com

San Diego County:
LifeScore
8899 University Center Lane, Suite 100
San Diego, CA 92122
Phone: 858–558–7267

Colorado
Colorado Heart Imaging
2490 W. 26th Avenue, Suite 120A
Denver, CO 80211–5801
Phone: 303–433–8800

Florida
Mount Sinai Cardiac Prevention Center
4300 Alton Road
Miami Beach, FL 33160
Phone: 305–674–3278

BodyScan – Orlando
3872 Oakwater Circle
Orlando, FL 32806
Phone: 407–851–9199

Health Test Scan
301 Yamato Road, Suite 1245
Boca Raton, FL 33431
Phone: 561–241-9299

Florida Institute Cardiovascular Care
700 North Hiatus Road, Suite 105
Pembroke Pines, FL 33026
Phone: 954-442-0879

BodyScan – Sarasota
3982 Bee Ridge Road, Building H
Sarasota, FL 34233
Phone: 941–929–0148

BodyScan – Tampa
3424 West Kennedy Boulevard
Tampa, FL 33609
Phone: 813–872–6391

Georgia
Lifetest Cardiac Imaging
Building I, Suite 9120
1140 Hammond Drive
Atlanta, GA 30328
Phone: 770–730–0119

Hawaii
Holistica Hawaii
Hilton Hawaiian Village
2005 Kalia Road
Honolulu, HI 96815–1999
Phone: 808–951–6546

Illinois
University of Illinois Physicians Group
2010 South Arlington Heights Road
Suite 104
Arlington Heights, IL 60005
Phone: 1–800–NEW–TEST

Rush Heart Scan
1725 West Harrison Avenue, Suite 025
Chicago, IL 60612
Phone: 1– 800–SCAN–123

University of Illinois Hospital
1740 W. Taylor Street, Suite 2101
Chicago, IL 60612
Phone: 1–800–NEW–TEST

BroMenn HeartCheck America
401 North Veterans Parkway
Bloomington, IL 61704
Phone: 309–268–3555

Edward Cardiovascular Institute
120 Spalding Drive, Suite 102
Naperville, IL 60540–6508
Phone: 630–527–2802

UltraFast HeartScan at Health Track
875 Roosevelt Road
Glen Ellyn, IL 60137
Phone: 630–545–3782

Prairie Heart Hospital
619 E. Mason Street
Springfield, IL 62701
Phone: 217–528–4633

Indiana
Rapid Scan
St. Joseph Regional Medical Center
801 East La Salle Avenue
South Bend, IN 46634
Phone: 219–280–5772

The Care Group
8333 Naab Road
Indianapolis, IN 46260
Phone: 317–338–6236

Iowa
The University of Iowa Hospitals & Clinics
Department of Radiology
200 Hawkins Drive
Iowa City, IA 52242–1009
Phone: 319–356–3444

Kansas
Midwest EBT Cardiac Imaging
7521 West 119th
Overland Park, KS 66213
Phone: 913–469–5958

Kentucky
Owensboro Heart and Vascular
1200 Breckenridge Street, Suite 101
Owensboro, KY 42303
Phone: 270–683–8672

Intecardia LifeCare Imaging
6420 Dutchmans Parkway, Suite 185
Louisville, KY 40205
Phone: 502–721–9898

Maryland
Maryland Heart Health
110 W. Timonium Road
Timonium, MD 21093
Phone: 410–453–0800

Minnesota
HeartScan Minnesota
Minneapolis Heart Institute &
Abbott Northwestern Hospital
Department of Radiology
800 East 28th Street
Minneapolis, MN 55407
Phone: 612–863–3500

Mayo Clinic
Rochester Methodist Hospital
Charlton Building
Rochester, MN 55905

Michigan
Michigan Heart Imaging
G3239 Beecher Road
Flint, MI 48532
Phone: 810–733–6182

Early Warning Healthcare Institute
3100 Cross Creek Parkway, Suite 160
Auburn Hills, MI 48326
Phone: 248–371–9000

EBT Heart & Body Imaging
26400 W. 12th Mile Road, Suite 114+
Southfield, MI 48034
Phone: 248–358–3225

Missouri
BodyScan – Kansas City
601 Westport
Kansas City, MO 64111
Phone: 816–931–2639

Heart Check St. Louis
522 North New Ballas Road, Suite 113
Creve Coeur, MO 63141
Phone: 800–NEW–TEST

Midwest Imaging and Prevention
605 Old Ballas Road, Suite 250
St. Louis, MO 63141
Phone: 314–997–3228

Nebraska
LifeScan Preventative Imaging
2930 Pine Lake Road, Suite 111
Lincoln, NE 68516
Phone: 402–420–7999

Nevada
HeartScan – Las Vegas
2400 Tech Center Court
Las Vegas, NV 89128
Phone: 702–256–8282

BodyScan – Las Vegas
2558 Wigwam Parkway
Henderson, NV 89014
Phone: 702–617–4518

New Jersey
Hackensack University Medical Center
Preventive Cardiology Program
20 Prospect Avenue, Suite 200
Hackensack, NJ 07601
Phone: 201–996–3802

Intecardia LifeCare Imaging
3 Sheila Drive
Tinton Falls, NJ 07724
Phone: 732–345–0900

Princeton Longevity Center
46 Vreeland Drive
Skillman, NJ 08558
Phone: 609–430–0752

New York
BodyScan Manhattan
301 East 55th Street
New York, NY 10022
Phone: 212–829–1177

Central Imaging
445 Kings Highway
Brooklyn, NY 11223
Phone: 866–886–7226

BodyScan Westchester
2975 Westchester Avenue
Purchase, NY 10577
Phone: 914–697–9500
Fax: 914–697–9507

Imaging for Life, LLC
4 Lyons Place
White Plains, NY 10601
Phone: 914–993–9600

St. Francis Hospital
DeMatteis Center for Research & Education
100 Port Washington Boulevard
Roslyn, NY 11576
Phone: 516–629–2000

University Heart Scan
307 East 63rd Street
New York, NY 10021
Phone: 877–576–7226

Inner Imaging
67 Irving Place
New York, NY 10003
Phone: 212–777–8900

Ohio
HealthWise Center
5747 Perimeter Drive, Suite 105
Dublin, OH 43017
Phone: 614–652–5888

Oregon
Heart Institute of the Cascades
2500 NE Neff Road
Bend, OR 97701–6015
Phone: 541–382–4321, ext. 2065

Pennsylvania
University of Pittsburgh Medical Center
Preventative Heart Care Center
120 Lytton Avenue, Suite 302
Pittsburgh, PA 15213–2593
Phone: 412–683–5580

HeartCam
Preventative Heart Care Center
3 Philadelphia Heart Institute Building
39th Street and Market
Philadelphia, PA 19104
Phone: 1–800–683–6942
          1–866–4HRTCAM

Mercy Heart Institute
Department of Radiology
1400 Locust Street
Pittsburgh, PA 15219–5166
Phone: 1–800–NEW–TEST

Philadelphia LifeScans –
Advanced Body and Cardiac Imaging
150 Monument Drive, Suite 105
Bala Cynwyd, PA 19004
Phone: 610–784–1900

Tennessee
LifeTest Cardiac Imaging
330 23th Avenue North
Nashville, TN 37203
Phone: 615–321–5700

Texas
The Heart Hospital of Austin
HeartSavers CT
3801 N. Lamar Boulevard
Austin, TX 78756
Phone: 512–407–7283

Cooper Clinic South
Department of Radiology
12200 Preston Road
Dallas, TX 75230
Phone: 972–239–7223

Cooper Clinic North
North Building
12200 Preston Road
Dallas, TX 75230
Phone: 972–560–2704

Heart Center
2301 West Wall Street, Suite 101
Midland, TX 79701
Phone: 915–687–3701
Fax: 915–687–3595

HeartScan – Houston
Scurlock Tower, Suite 610
6560 Fannin Street
Houston, TX 77030
Phone: 713–796–8940

Houston Preventative Imaging
8800 Katy Freeway, Suite 105
Houston, TX 77024
Phone: 713–436–9090

University of Texas Southwest
5801 Forest Park Rogers, MRI Building
Dallas, TX 75235
Phone: 214–648–5800

ViaScan of Las Colinas
349 Las Colinas Boulevard, Suite C
Irving, TX 75039
Phone: 800–585–2702
Fax: 972–739–2854

Covenant EBT
3615 19th Street
Lubbock, TX 79410
Phone 806–725–2328

Virginia
Intecardia LifeCare Imaging
7229 Forest Avenue, Suite 108
Richmond, VA 23226
Phone: 804–285–SCAN

Washington
Swedish Heart Institute EBT Services
Swedish Medical Center
Providence Campus
500 17th Avenue
Seattle, WA 98124
Phone: 206–320–4411

Washington, DC
Heart Check Washington DC
2401 Pennsylvania Avenue NW
Washington, DC 20037
Phone: 202–467–0929

Wisconsin
Milwaukee Heart Scan
10200 Innovation Drive, Suite 600
Milwaukee, WI 53226
Phone: 414–774–7600

EBT scanner

Addendum B
Useful Web Sites

ocheartdiet.com
Source for other information on **The OC Heart Diet** and for information on ordering books.

ocheart.org
Source for information on Orange County Heart Institute, Orange, California

ocvitalimaging.com
Leading EBCT center in Orange County, California.

megaheart.com
Leading source for low salt cooking and baking

berkeleyheartlabs.com
Source for information on advanced lipid testing

cardiorei.edu/ufct.com
Leading EBCT center in Los Angeles County, California

atherotech.com
Source for information on advanced lipid testing

webmd.com
Source for medical references

americanheart.org
American Heart Association

cardiosource.com
American College of Cardiology

invisionguide.com
Video and text information on the human heart

innerbody.com
Human anatomy online

sln.fi.edu/biosci/heart.html
The Franklin Institute Science Museum

medtropolis.com/VBody.asp
Three-part interactive exploration of the human heart

cdc.gov/nccdphp
National Center for Health Statistics

Addendum C
References

1. Santora L, Marin J, Vangrow J, Minegar C, Robinson M, Mora J, Friede G. "Coronary Calcification in Anabolic Steroid Users. Submitted for publication 2005.

2. Arad Y, Spadaro LA, Goodman K, et al. "Predictive value of electron beam computed tomography of the coronary arteries. 19-month follow-up of 1,173 asymptomatic subjects." *Circulation* 1996; 93:1951–3.

3. Arad Y, Spadaro LA, Goodman K, Newstein D, Cuerci AD. "Prediction of coronary events with electron beam computed tomography." *J Am Coll Cardiol* 2000; 36:1253–60.

4. Wong ND, Hsu JC, Detrano RC, Diamond G, Eisenberg H, Gardin JM. "Coronary artery calcium evaluation by electron beam computed tomography and its relation to new cardiovascular events." *Am J Cardiol* 2000; 86:495–8.

5. Raggi P, Callister TQ, Cooil B, et al. "Identification of patients at increased risk of first unheralded acute myocardial infarction by electron-beam computed tomography." *Circulation* 2000; 101:850–5.

6. Keelan PC, Bielak LF, Ashai K, et al. "Long-term prognostic value of coronary calcification detected by electron-beam computed tomography in patients undergoing coronary angiography." *Circulation* 2001; 104:412–7.

7. Raggi P, Cooil B, Callister TQ. "Use of electron beam tomography data to develop models for prediction of hard coronary events." *Am Heart J* 2001; 141:375–82.

8. Park R, Detrano R, Xiang M, et al. "Combined use of computed tomography coronary calcium scores and C-reactive protein levels in predicting cardiovascular events in nondiabetic individuals." *Circulation* 2002; 106:2073–7.

9. Vliegenthart R, Oudkerk M, Song B, van der Kuip DA, Hofman A, Witteman JC. "Coronary calcification detected by electron-beam computed tomography and myocardial infarction." *The Rotterdam Coronary Calcification Study. Eur Heart J* 2002; 23:1596–603.

10. Kondos GT, Hoff JA, Sevrukov A, et al. "Electron-beam tomography coronary artery calcium and cardiac events: a 37-month follow-up of 5,635 initially asymptomatic low- to intermediate-risk adults." *Circulation* 2003; 107:2571–6.

11. Shaw LJ, Raggi P, Schisterman E, Berman DS. Callister TQ. "Prognostic value of cardiac risk factors and coronary artery calcium screening for all-cause mortality." *Radiology* 2003; 228:826–33.

12. Ladenheim ML, Pollock BH, Rozanski A, et al. "Extent and severity of myocardial hypoperfusion as predictors of prognosis in patients with suspected coronary artery disease." *J Am Coll Cardiol* 1986; 7:464–71.

13. Staniloff HM, Forrester JS, Berman DS, Swan HJ. "Prediction of death, myocardial infarction, and worsening chest pain using thallium scintigraphy and exercise electrocardiography." *J Nuel Med* 1986; 27:1842–8.

14. Brown KA. "Prognostic value of thallium-201 myocardial perfusion imaging. A diagnostic tool comes of age." *Circulation* 1991; 83:363–81.

15. Iskandrian AS, Chae SC, Heo J, Stanberry CD, Wasserleben V, Cave V. "Independent and incremental prognostic value of exercise single-photon emission computed tomographic (SPECT) thallium imaging in coronary artery disease." *J Am Coll Cardiol* 1993; 22:665–70.

16. Hachamovitch R, Berman DS, Kiat H, et al. "Exercise myocardial perfusion SPECT in patients without known coronary artery disease: incremental prognostic value and use in risk stratification." *Circulation* 1996; 93:905–14.

17. Hachamovitch R, Berman DS, Shaw LJ, et al. "Incremental prognostic value of myocardial perfusion single photon emission computed tomography for the prediction of cardiac death: differential stratification for risk of cardiac death and myocardial infarction." *Circulation* 1998; 97:535–43.

18. Hachamovitch R, Hayes SW, Friedman JD, Cohen L, Berman DS. "Stress myocardial perfusion SPECT is clinically effective and cost-effective in risk-stratification of patients with a high likelihood of CAD but no known CAD." *J Am Coll Cardiol* 2004; 43:200–8.

19. Poornima IG, Miller TD, Christian TF, Hodge DO, Bailey KR, Gibbons RJ. "Utility of myocardial perfusion imaging in patients with low-risk treadmill scores." *J Am Coll Cardiol* 2004; 43:194–9.

20. Timmis AD, Lutkin JE, Fenney LJ, et al. "Comparison of dipyridamole and treadmill exercise for enhancing thallium-201 perfusion defects in patients with coronary artery disease." *Eur Heart J* 1980; 1:275–80.

21. Narita M, Kurihara T, Usami M. "Noninvasive detection of coronary artery disease by myocardial imaging with thallium-201—the significance of pharmacologic interventions." *Jpn Circ J* 1981; 45:127–40.

22. Varma SK, Watson DD, Beller GA. "Quantitative comparison of thallium-201 scintigraphy after exercise and dipyridamole in coronary artery disease." *Am J Cardiol* 1989; 64:871–7.

23. Wong ND, Sciammarella MG, Polk D, et al. "The metabolic syndrome, diabetes and subclinical atherosclerosis assessed by coronary calcium." *J Am Coll Cardiol* 2003; 41:1547–53.

24. Diamond GA, Staniloff HM, Forrester JS, Pollock BH, Swan HJ. "Computer-assisted diagnosis in the noninvasive evaluation of patients with suspected coronary artery disease." *J Am Coll Cardiol* 1983; 1:444–55.

25. Raggi P. "Prognostic implications of absolute and relative calcium scores." *Herz* 2001; 26:252–9.

26. Kajinami K, Seki H, Takekoshi N, Mabuchi H. "Noninvasive prediction of coronary atherosclerosis by quantification of coronary artery calcification using electron beam computed tomography: comparison with electrocardiographic and thallium exercise stress test results." *J Am Coll Cardiol* 1995; 6:1209–21.

27. Schmermund A, Baumgart D, Sack S, et al. "Assessment of coronary calcification by electron-beam computed tomography in symptomatic patients with normal, abnormal, or equivocal exercise stress test." *Eur Heart J* 2000; 21:1674–82.

28. Shavelle DM, Budoff MJ, LaMont DH, Shavelle RM, Kennedy JM, Brundage BH. "Exercise testing and electron beam computed tomography in the evaluation of coronary artery disease." *J Am Coll Cardiol* 2000; 36:32–8.

29. Schmermund A, Denktas AE, Rumberger JA, et al. "Independent and incremental value of coronary artery calcium for predicting the extent of angiographic coronary artery disease: comparison with cardiac risk factors and radionuclide perfusion imaging." *J Am Coll Cardiol* 1999; 34:777–86.

30. He ZX, Hedrick TD, Pratt CM, et al. "Severity of coronary artery calcification by electron beam computed tomography predicts silent myocardial ischemia." *Circulation* 2000; 101:244–51.

31. Vijayaraghavan K, Singh-Khalsa M, Asher R, et al. "Relationship of coronary ischemia by nuclear imaging and coronary artery calcification by electron beam tomography in asymptomatic patients (abstr)." *J Nucl Caroiol* 2003; 10:F16.

32. Klocke FJ, Baird MC, Lorell BH, et al. "ACC/AHA/ASNC guidelines for the clinical use of cardiac radionuclide imaging-executive summary: a report of the American College of Cardiology/American Heart Association Task Force on Practice Guidelines" (ACC/AHA/ASNC Committee to Revise the 1995 Guidelines for the Clinical Use of Cardiac Radionuclide Imaging). *J Am Coll Cardiol* 2003; 42:1318–33.

33. Brown BG, Zhao XQ, Chait A, et al. "Simvastatin and niacin, antioxidant vitamins, or the combination for the prevention of coronary disease." *N Engl J Med* 2001; 345:1583–1592.

34. Law MR, Wald NJ, Rudnick AR. "Quantifying the effect of statins on low density lipoprotein cholesterol, ischaemic heart disease, and stroke." *BMJ* 2003; 326:1423–1430.

35. Azen SP, Mack WJ, Cashin-Hemphill L, et al. "Progression of coronary artery disease predicts clinical coronary events." *Circulation* 1996; 93:34–41.

36. Arad Y, Spadaro LA, Roth M, Newstein D, Guerci AD. "Treatment of asymptomatic adults with elevated coronary calium scores with atorvastatin, vitamin C, and vitamin E: the St. Francis Heart Study randomized clinical trial."*J Am Coll Cardiol.* 2005; 46:166 –172.

37. Rasouli ML, Nasir K, Blumenthal RS, Park R, Aziz DC, Budoff MJ. "Plasma homocysteine predicts progression of atherosclerosis". *Atherosclerosis.* 2005 Jul; 181(1):159-65.

38. Taylor AJ, Bindeman J, Feuerstein I, Cao F, Brazaitis M,O'Malley PG. "Coronary calcium independently predicts incident premature coronary heart disease over measured cardiovascular risk factors: mean three-year outcomes in the Prospective Army Coronary Calcium (PACC) project."*J Am Coll Cardiol.* 2005 Sep6; 46(5):807-14.

39. Arad Y, Goodman KJ, Roth M, Newstein D, Guerci AD. "Coronary calcification, coronary disease risk factors, C-reactive protein, and atherosclerotic cardiovascular disease events: the St. Francis Heart Study". *J Am Coll Cardiol.* 2005 Jul 5; 46(1):158-65.

40. Budoff MJ, Chen GP, Hunter CJ, Takasu J, Agrawal N, Sorochinsky B, Mao S. *"Effects of hormone replacement on progression of coronary calcium as measured by electron beam tomography."J Womens Health (Larchmt).* 2005,Jun;14(5):410-7.

41. LaMonte MJ, FitzGerald SJ, Church TS, Barlow CE, Radford NB, Levine BD, Pippin JJ, Gibbons LW, Blair SN, Nichaman MZ. "Coronary artery calcium score and coronary heart disease events in a large cohort of asymptomatic men and women." *AmJEpidemiol.*2005Sep1;162(5):421-9.Epub 005Aug2.

42. Shemesh J, Koren-Morag N, Apter S, Rozenman J, Kirwan BA, Itzchak Y, Motro M." Accelerated progression of coronary calci fication: four-year follow-up in patients with stable coronaryarterydisease."*Radiology.*2004Oct;233(1):201- Epub2004Aug27.

43. Michos ED, Vasamreddy CR, Becker DM, Yanek LR, Moy TF, Fishman EK, Becker LC, Blumenthal RS. "Women with a low Framingham risk score and a family history of premature coronary heart disease have a high prevalence of subclinical coronary atherosclerosis." *Am Heart J.* 2005 Dec; 150(6):1276- 81.

44. Solfrizzi V, Capurso C, Colacicco AM, D'Introno A, Fontana C, Capurso SA, Torres F, Gadaleta AM, Koverech A, Capurso A, Panza F. "Efficacy and tolerability of combined treatment with l-carnitine and simvastatin in lowering lipoprotein(a) serum levels in patients with type 2 diabetes mellitus." *Atherosclerosis.* 2005 Dec 26; [Epub ahead of print]

45. Dreon DM, Fernstrom HA, Williams PT, Krauss RM. A very low fat diet is not associated with improved lipoprotein profiles in men with a predominace of large LDLs. Circulation 1996;94:I-96.

46. Lamarche B, Tchernof A, Mauriege P, Cantin B, Dagenais R, Lupien PJ, Despres JP. Fasting insulin and apolipoprotein B levels and low-density lipoprotein particle size as risk factors for ischemic heart disease. JAMA1998;279:1955-1961.

47. Lamarche B, Tchernof A, Mauriege P, Cantin B, Dagenais GR, Lupien PJ, Despres JP. Fasting insulin and apolipoprotein B levels and low-density lipoprotein particle size as risk factor for ischemic heart disease. JAMA 1998;279:1955-1961.)

48. Desmarais, Rene L; Sarembock, Ian J, et al. Elevated Serum Lipoprotein(a) Is a Risk Factor for Clinical Recurrence afterBalloon Angioplasty.Circulation. 1995;91:1403-1409.)

49. Mack WJ, Krauss RM, Hodis HN. Lipoprotein subclasses inthe Monitored Atherosclerosis Regression Study (MARS). Arterioscler Thromb Vasc Biol 16 1996;16:697-704.)

Addendum D

The OC Heart Diet
Food Categories and Exchange List

Following, is a list of acceptable foods that you can use in the different meals of your personal plan to increase variety. Just remember that, unless otherwise shown, the figures that you see in grams of protein, carbohydrates, and fats are for one ounce servings. Following the exchange list is easy. Look at your personalized menu. See how many grams of protein, carbohydrate, or fat you are supposed to have per meal. Then look on the exchange list and find the item that you would like to substitute. If it is a protein, for instance, see how many ounces are needed to meet your protein requirements for that meal. Divide the grams of protein per meal by the number of grams of protein in one serving of the food you are substituting.

For example, if the meal you choose has twenty grams of protein, and the menu has fish, but you would like to substitute lamb, then follow the exchange list and find lamb. Lamb has 7.5 grams protein per ounce. Your meal calls for 20 grams of protein. To get closest to 20 grams of protein in lamb, divide 20 by 7.5 = about 3 ounces of lamb. The same applies for carbohydrates and fats. We also listed normal serving size amounts—just to make it a little easier for you—in the carbs section.

50% Low Glycemic Carbohydrates
We need 50% of our food to be low-glycemic to medium-glycemic carbohydrates. The vegetables, fruits, and other carbohydrates listed on your menu and in this exchange list won't cause rapid

increases in your blood sugar levels. Remember surges in blood sugar levels from high-glycemic foods cause insulin levels to rise, then a subsequent drop in blood sugar. In other words, a relatively steady level of blood sugar will keep your energy levels up throughout the day and you will avoid the late afternoon fatigue that often accompanies high-glycemic meals.

Vegetables

You can consume an unlimited quantities of vegetables. These vitamins, mineral and fiber-rich foods can only enhance your cardiovascular health. The additions that kill these healthy foods are dips, butter, cheeses, and unhealthy dressings. Just eat them without dressings other than olive oil and other mono-saturated oil dressings and enjoy all the individual flavors.

Fruits

If you can have 40 grams of carbs per meal, you only get two (2) whole fruits. Sometimes not even that. Berries, on the other hand, are the best. You can eat 16 ounces (two cups) and only get about 40 grams of carbs. That's a lot of berries and a whopping amount of fiber!

Breads, Pasta and Rice:

Breads, cereals, rice, pastas, potatoes, muffins, crackers, cakes and others are the biggest challenge. So, except on special occasions, pretty much avoid these foods unless one is specifically listed in your menu plan. Whole grain bread, whole grain pastas brown rice, instead of white rice, yams and sweet potato instead of white potato are the lower glycemic choices when you do have to eat these foods.

25% Protein

Your body cannot function at its peak without 25% protein in your diet. Your moods, energy levels both mental and physical are all affected by when, how often and how much protein you eat. It's that simple.

Often we eat way too much protein: 20-ounce steaks, 1/2 chickens, triple-decker hamburgers, slabs of barbeque ribs, etc., etc., etc. However, eating the correct quantity and proportion of protein every three to four hours is much more effective for endurance, strength and energy than large quantities of protein consumed at one meal. It really works!

Most proteins; i.e., meat, seafood, fowl, cottage cheese, and eggs have enough fat in them. So, unless you're making a protein fruit smoothie, you don't need any additional fat like sauces, butter, margarine, salad dressings, etc. Make sure to get quality protein (just check the exchange list) every meal. And, double check on that portion size

Also be aware that not all protein sources are the same. Some proteins are better quality, meaning they are readily absorbed and utilized by your body (high bio-availability). Some proteins are poorly utilized by your body and do not contain all the essential amino acids.(low bio-availability). Both types of protein are healthy, however, the high bio-available proteins are just better utilized for muscle building and repair.

25% Essential Fats

Some fats are actually necessary for life. These good, friendly fats are called Essential Fats. We need about 25% of each meal to contain some of these. You'll see them in the exchange list as preferred fat. Eat these whenever possible. However, keep one thing in mind, even though there are a lot of good fats (see the food exchange list) even a large person only needs 3 or 4 tablespoons total per day. So be really careful when it comes to fat intake. It likes to hide in little packages everywhere and, until you know where to look, use our little guide.

Even though our menu plans have pretty good examples of what your portion sizes should be, you can really add variety by using the exchange list as often as you want. It just gives you more choices and more ways to enjoy food.

Exchange List

Carbohydrates
Preferred

Vegetables

Low Glycemic Rating
(1 oz unless indicated)

	Serving Size	Grams Carbs
Asparagus	(1 spear)	.5
Beans (string)		.4
Beets		1.4
Broccoli		1.0
Brussel sprouts		1.6
Cabbage		1.0
Carrot	(1 medium)	3.6
Cauliflower		.6
Celery		.4
Cucumber		.5
Eggplant		.8
Sugar snap peas		1.1
Lettuce (any)		.3
Mixed vegetables		2.5
Mushrooms (raw)		.4
Mushrooms (cooked)		1.0
Onions (raw)		1.5
Onions (cooked)		1.7
Peas		2.6
Peppers (sweet, bell)		.6
Red cabbage		.6
Spinach (raw)		.2
Spinach (cooked)		.8
Squash		.5
Tomato (large)		8.0
Water chestnuts		2.2
Zucchini		.5

Fruits – fresh

Medium Glycemic Rating

	Serving Size	Grams Carbs
Apple	(1 medium)	23.0
Apricot	(1 medium)	4.0
Banana	(1, not too ripe)	26.0
Berries	(1/2 cup)	10.0
Cantaloupe	(1/4)	11.0
Grapes	(1 cup)	15.0
Honeydew	(2 inch slice)	23.0
Kiwi	(one)	11.0
Mango	(1/2)	17.0
Mixed fruits	(1/2 cup)	10.0
Nectarine	(one)	16.0
Orange	(one)	15.0
Papaya	(one)	30.0
Peach	(one)	10.0
Pear	(one)	25.0
Pineapple	(1 cup)	19.0
Plums	(one)	9.0
Raisins	(1 oz)	22.6
Tangerine	(one)	10.0
Watermelon	(1 cup)	12.0

Breads

	Serving Size	Grams Carbs
Pita	(one whole)	34.0
Pumpernickel	(one slice)	15.0
Stone ground wheat	(100%-one slice)	15.0
Sourdough	(one slice)	20.0

Breakfast Cereals

Low to Medium Glycemic Rating

	Serving Size	Grams Carbs
All Bran	(1/2 cup)	20.0
Bran Flakes	(1/2 cup)	19.0
Cheerios	(1 cup)	16.0
Meusli (natural)	(1/2 cup)	14.0
Oatmeal	(1/2 cup)	12.0
Shredded Wheat	(spoonsize-2/3 cup)	27.0
Special K	(1 cup)	22.0
Total	(1 cup)	22.0

Rice - cooked
Low to Medium Glycemic Rating

	Serving Size	Grams Carbs
White	(1 cup)	42.0
Brown	(1 cup)	37.0
Uncle Ben's	(converted-1 cup)	38.0

Pasta - cooked
Low Glycemic Rating

	Serving Size	Grams Carbs
Fettucini/Linguine	(1 cup)	57.0
Macaroni	(1 cup)	52.0
Ravioli	(cheese/meat-1 cup)	32.0
Spaghetti	(1 cup)	52.0
Vermicelli	(1 cup)	46.4

Potatoes
Low to Medium Glycemic Rating

	Serving Size	Grams Carbs
New Red with skin	(5 small)	23.0
Sweet	(1/2 cup mashed)	20.0
Yams	(1/2 cup mashed)	25.0

Muffins
Low to Medium Glycemic Rating

	Serving Size	Grams Carbs
Apple cinnamon	(1/2)	33.0
Banana oat honey	(1/2)	27.0
Blueberry	(1/2)	27.0
Oat bran	(1/2)	28.0

Crackers
Low to Medium Glycemic Rating

	Serving Size	Grams Carbs
Wheat Thins	(16 crackers)	21.0
Soda	5 crackers)	13.0

Cakes
Low to Medium Glycemic Rating

	Serving Size	Grams Carbs
Angel food	(1 slice)	14.0
Banana bread	(1/2 slice)	15.0
Pound cake	(1/2 slice)	14.0

Other
Low to Medium Glycemic Rating

	Serving Size	Grams Carbs
Popcorn (light)	(2 cups)	12.0
Pretzels, hard	(about 3)	22.0

Proteins

High bio-availability

	Grams Pro	Grams Fat
Meat		
Beef (1 ounce)		
Filet, porterhouse, T-bone, etc	5.5	4.5
Lean cuts	8.0	3.5
Lean hamburger	5.5	4.5
Veal	6.0	4.0
Lamb	7.5	3.5
Pork (1 ounce)		
Loin	5.5	3.5
Leg (roasted)	5.5	3.0
Steak	5.0	1.0
Ham	5.0	1.3
Fowl		
Chicken (1 ounce)		
Breast (no skin)	6.4	1.2
Dark meat (no skin)	5.3	1.2
White meat canned	6.4	.8
Turkey (1 ounce)		
Breast (no skin)	9.25	1.0
Ground	7.0	.4
Dark Meat	6.0	1.2
Seafood		
Fish (1 ounce)		
Salmon	5.3	1.8
Swordfish	5.2	1.1
Halibut	7.4	.8
Sole	4.0	.2
Trout	5.8	1.0
Orange Roughy	4.2	2.0
Tuna (water packed)	8.0	.5

Ahi	6.4	.15
Whitefish	5.0	1.6

Shellfish (1 ounce)

Crabmeat	5.0	.3
Lobster	6.0	.1
Oysters	3.0	.6
Scallops	4.0	.05
Shrimp	5.3	.5

Dairy (1/2 cup)

Cottage cheese (2%)	14	2.5
Cottage cheese (1%)	14	1.5

Eggs

Whole egg (large)	6.5	4.0
Egg white (large)	6.5	0

Proteins

Lesser bio-availability

	Grams Carbs	Grams Pro	Grams Fat
Soy (1 ounce)	.5	2.3	1.0
Legumes (1 ounce)			
Beans (average)	.5	2.0	25
Lentils	.5	2.3	.4
Yogurt			
(1 cup non-fat plain)	17.0	13.0	.5
Low fat milk (1 cup)	8.0	12.0	4.7
Non fat milk (1 cup)	12.0	12.0	0
Parmesan cheese (2 oz)	10.0	1.0	7.0

Fats

Preferred

	Grams Fat
Polyunsaturated (1Tbsp)	10
Monounsaturated (1Tbsp)	
Canola	10
Olive	10
Peanut	10
Sesame	10
Walnut	10

Unsatisfactory fats

Saturated (1Tbsp)	
Butter	10
Coconut	10
Lard	10
Palm oil	10

Afterword

The Mean and Clean Campaign

After Dick Butkus discovered his own heart disease, he became a strong advocate of early detection of heart disease, in adults as well adolescents. A recent study using EBCT heart scans performed by The Orange County Heart Institute on professional body builders using steroids, confirmed a high prevalence of premature hardening of the coronary arteries. The *Mean and Clean* campaign was created to address the endemic problem of steroid abuse among young athletes. Experts estimate that 5 to 6% of the total population of high school students has abused steroids. That's about 1 million of our children each year. Regular steroid use can lead to heart disease, cancer and liver damage and other physical problems plus emotional effects like depression and "roid rage". Butkus spoke directly to high school players about steroids in his ESPN reality show *Bound for Glory* that aired this fall and the *Mean and Clean* campaign will maximize this effort on a national level. *Team Butkus* intends to reach out to a broad spectrum of support from Congress, the business community, Hollywood and all the major sports leagues for support for the *Mean and Clean* campaign. The goal is to increase awareness of the serious health consequences of steroid use and to provide educational material to every high school athlete in America delivering a strong, positive, anti-steroid message.

According to Butkus "There is a myth out there that somehow steroids can turn a cub into a bear..... steroids won't make you tough; it's that simple"...and there are few who know more about being tough than the most feared player in the history of professional football. The name Butkus has been synonymous with the word 'tough' for more than 40 years. "If every football team had a linebacker like Dick Butkus, all fullbacks would soon be three feet tall and sing soprano," wrote Dan Jenkins in Sports Illustrated. Butkus was aptly described as "Moby Dick in a sea of guppies".

The standard by which linebackers are measured is defined by the Butkus Award, given each year to the nation's best college football linebacker. Dick Butkus was inducted into the Professional Football Hall of Fame only six years after he retired from his legendary career with the Chicago Bears. After repeated appearances as the starting Middle-Linebacker in the NFL Pro-Bowl, he was selected to the NFL's "All-Time Team". Other football awards include being named a six-time "All NFL Linebacker", a two-time "NFC Defensive Player of the Year", and "Pro-Football's All-Time Greatest Linebacker" by the fans of The Sporting News. In tribute to his life off the field, Butkus was presented with the Life Time Achievement Award from Cedars-Sinai Medical Center in Los Angeles and he is the recipient of the "Pope John Award", which recognizes outstanding achievement towards humanity.

Today, the Butkus image continues to resonate with fathers and sons a quarter of a century after his retirement. Dick Butkus is a living American icon for toughness, competitiveness and individualism-a hero for sports fans. No other player possesses the legacy, the enduring mystique or the level of authenticity of a real American football hero for the working class. The Butkus name is transcendent because he is the genuine article

It is not surprising that as Butkus has moved forward in life. He has attacked fitness and health with the same energy and relentlessness that made him a legend on the football field. Several years ago, Butkus learned that he was suffering from cardiovascular disease and after having a successful surgical intervention he teamed up with the world-class physicians who saved his life to develop a lifestyle modification program. This program addressed the concerns of nutrition, exercise and stress management and his rehabilitation was remarkable. Butkus lost 35 pounds and regained the fitness profile of a man decades younger. This program is now available in *The O C Heart Diet.*

About Dr. Armentrout

Dr. Armentrout is a leading physician in the field of internal medicine. He served as a faculty member in several universities, including the University of California at Irvine, and has participated as an investigator in a number of areas related to better eating. As a prolific writer he is well qualified to advise readers on the proper diet for most any condition, particularly heart patients. He continues with research and writing in his field of oncology with emphasis on diet, having served on the Food and Drug Administration, Research Review Committee. He is eminently qualified to give the best advice for a healthy diet.

About Dick Butkus

Dick Butkus played in eight Pro Bowls and the acclaim he gained went far beyond his hometown of Chicago; it reached legendary status. Until he submitted to an EBCT full body scans, detailed here, he had no idea of a heart problem. "The heart scan saved my life," he said. "The full body scan revealed that I had a serious heart condition with one foot in the grave and other on a banana peel." Shortly after his scan he had a 5-way bypass operation that may have saved his life. Today, he is a vigorous, active person who speaks throughout the nation touting the need for care of the body and vital heart tests. In this book he relates his success at better health.

About Dr. Santora

D r. Santora is in private cardiology prac tice in Orange County, California where he lives with his family. He is a member of the *Orange County Heart Institute and Research Center.*

Dr. Santora did his undergraduate training at the University of Miami, Florida, then went on to receive his medical degree from New York Medical College. His cardiology training and Cardiology Fellowship were completed at the University of California at Irvine.

In the area of research, Dr. Santora was involved in studying the effects of liquid protein diets on cardiac function and heart rhythms in obese patients. Subsequent interests involved various studies on heart rhythm and defibrillators. He is currently involved in research using ECP (external conterpulsation, a non-invasive treatment for angina). Recent results have shown the benefit of ECP for congestive heart failure patients. He is involved in EBCT heart scans to evaluate the effects of steroid use in elite body-builders. The results show an alarmingly high development of hardening of the coronary arteries in steroid users at a relatively young age.

Though actively pursuing interventional cardiology, he continues to maintain his interests in heart disease detection and prevention.

If you wish to order this book on line, go to the following web address: http://www.ocheartdiet.com.

Look for the soon-to-be-released books by the cardiologists of the Orange County Heart Institute: *Women and Heart Disease: A New Epidemic*, by Dr. Santora, Dr. Shokooh and Dr. Tucker. Also soon available, *A Cardiologist's Guide to Controlling High Blood Pressure,* by Dr. Azer and Dr. Santora. The *ocheart.org* web site will announce the release of these books.

Index

C

D

F

G

T

U

V

W

Y

Printed in the United States
45755LVS00003B/94-276